MID-AMERICA
TRIPS AND TRAILS

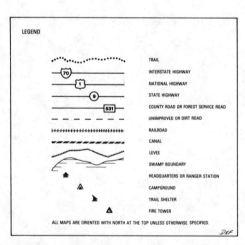

LEGEND

••••••••	TRAIL
70	INTERSTATE HIGHWAY
1	NATIONAL HIGHWAY
9	STATE HIGHWAY
531	COUNTY ROAD OR FOREST SERVICE ROAD
– – – –	UNIMPROVED OR DIRT ROAD
++++++++++++++	RAILROAD
▬▬▬▬▬	CANAL
⌂⌂⌂⌂⌂⌂	LEVEE
	SWAMP BOUNDARY
♠	HEADQUARTERS OR RANGER STATION
Δ	CAMPGROUND
▶	TRAIL SHELTER
▲	FIRE TOWER

ALL MAPS ARE ORIENTED WITH NORTH AT THE TOP UNLESS OTHERWISE SPECIFIED.

DKF

Maps by Dave Farlow; Lee Nading,
President, North American Trail
Complex; and Levon Coate

MID-AMERICA TRIPS AND TRAILS

Bill Thomas

Stackpole Books

MID-AMERICA TRIPS AND TRAILS

Copyright © 1975 by
Bill Thomas

Published by
STACKPOLE BOOKS
Cameron and Kelker Streets
Harrisburg, Pa. 17105

Printed in the U.S.A.

Library of Congress Cataloging in Publication Data

Thomas, Bill, 1934-
  Mid-America trips and trails.

  1. Outdoor recreation—Middle West. 2. Wilderness areas—Middle
West. 3. Camp sites, facilities, etc.—Middle West. 4. Trails—Middle
West. I. Title.
GV191.42.M53T48   917.6'04'4   74-34053
ISBN 0-8117-2037-3

Dedicated to Desiree

Contents

A Note of Appreciation

The author wishes to express his appreciation to the many officials and personnel of the Bureau of Sportfisheries and Wildlife who administer the national wildlife refuges, the U.S. Forest Service, the National Park Service, various state and local agencies and private citizens who helped with the compilation of this work. And to Phyllis, who helped with the research, and the late Desiree, who assisted, my special gratitude.

introduction

Along the bottomlands of the Wabash in southeastern Illinois is a small tract of virgin forestland called Beall Woods. Here in the fertile topsoil deposited by the river through the ages grow giant trees—poplar, oak, sycamore, walnut and hickory—that once covered a vast portion of Mid-America. This is a small but significant remaining segment of the forest primeval that our pioneer forefathers knew as they made their way westward from the barrier mountains to the east.

Just two centuries ago such a forest of magnificent hardwoods extended all the way from the Atlantic Ocean to the Mississippi and beyond to the Great Prairie—so dense a squirrel could span the entire distance and never touch ground. To walk through this 635-acre tract on the primitive trails provided today is an experience to be cherished forever. For Beall Woods—though small it is—represents wilderness, something which is becoming more and more difficult to find in Mid-America.

But it does exist. There are many places that still offer one an escape from the hectic pace of modern life, places where one may achieve a wilderness experience even though the croplands of the farmer's field or the industrial hum of factories may be only a short distance away. At Theodore Roosevelt National Park in North Dakota, for instance, one may sit for hours upon a knoll watching a black tide move across the land—a herd of buffalo grazing—reminiscent of a bygone era. And in the swamplands of Louisiana's Atchafalaya Basin, one can canoe among thick stands of bald cypress draped with strands of Spanish moss, can watch white egret and blue heron fish for their dinner or stand spellbound by a harvest moon glimmering on the murky morass.

One can become lost in the Atchafalaya and have to pit his skills in basic understanding of the outdoors and nature in order to find civilization once again. Thank God such places still exist in the midsection of America; let's hope they will forever so that our children and the children who follow them for all time to come shall be afforded the opportunity to experience what little wilderness there is left.

Henry David Thoreau, perhaps America's foremost naturalist of all time, wrote long before the turn of the century those immortal words: "In wilderness is the preservation of the world." And he was one of the first Americans to sense a threat to the remaining wilderness, even in the middle of the 19th century.

Wilderness is indeed part of the American heritage. This nation was spawned in wilderness, was carved from it at great effort and expense and, too often ruthless destruction. Those of us who live or have lived or traveled in that area of Mid-America stretching from Canada to the Gulf of Mexico and the Rio Grande Valley are well aware of that. For we can see the scars left by overgrazing, by relentless and unethical overuse of land and the utter disregard for those natural qualities that are so much a part of Mother Earth.

The remnants left in Mid-America whereby we may achieve a wilderness experience are comparatively few, yet their preservation is imperative if our society is to survive, if we are, in fact, to have a place where we can walk alone and examine ourselves and our natural environment, to stand tall and breathe deeply of fresh unpolluted air and renew our spirit, where we can gain new perspectives in our own lives. A wilderness encounter is a rare and perhaps an awesome occasion. Some claim it borders on religion, that it is for them a soul-lifting experience, a special commune with nature.

The Wilderness Act of 1964 provided the administrative-legislative mechanism to define and preserve the bits of wilderness left in the East and in Mid-America. And in 1974, the Eastern Wilderness Bill further outlined concepts and places of wilderness on public lands. This book is a work designed to provide the people with the location, description and means by which one may experience each chunk of wilderness in Mid-America and, in addition, informational contacts whereby you may expand your knowledge of these areas.

Some of the places included in this book have not actually been designated wilderness areas. In fact, Beall Woods is neither an official wilderness nor will you find a section on it in this book. It is listed, however, in the back so you may write for information and guidelines on how to get there and when to visit. All of the places included here—in one way or another—provide a true wilderness experience, however, and are worthy, in my estimation, of your investigation and further research. Some of them, under the guidelines prescribed by Congress, would never measure up. Some are too small, some possess other complications which detract from their worthiness for official wilderness designation. But discover them for yourself and let your imagination roam free, not in terms of what you have been told wilderness should be, but in terms of what you imagine it was like when your ancestors first walked this land.

Whether the areas included in this book have been officially designated as wilderness areas or not is of little importance. But it is important that they are comprised of the necessary ingredients that merit consideration as wilderness. And, hopefully, through public exposure enough pressure will be brought to bear to insure preservation of their natural state for posterity.

We have not gone into great detail or specifics of individual trails through wilderness areas here. We have provided instead the basic knowledge and concepts in the hope that the reader will be inspired to follow up his whims and desires to encounter such a wilderness experience, to learn firsthand what wilderness is really like, to explore, to come face to face with his neighbors of the wild kingdom.

Included herein are numerous tracts of natural beauty and places for a wilderness experience in seventeen states of Mid-America. Some are a part of the national wildlife refuges, some are in national forests, some are prairielands, and some are swamps. Some have placid streams and some dense stands of giant trees for wilderness comes in different packages . . . not necessarily wrapped with the same ribbon.

It is my sincere wish that the reader will visit and enjoy at least one of the wilderness areas herein described and that you find the experience most everlastingly rewarding.

MICHIGAN

big island lakes wilderness

IN THE HIAWATHA National Forest of Michigan's Upper Peninsula is the Big Island Lakes Wilderness, comprising 6,606 acres with 23 interrelated small lakes and streams nestled in birch-clad hills. With elevations ranging from 60 to 80 feet above the water, these hills provide great panoramic views of the surrounding landscape. Located just 15 miles from Lake Superior and 35 miles to the north of Lake Michigan, the area still shows strong signs of glaciated features.

The most picturesque of the lakes is Big Island Lake, itself, from which the area takes its name. Several of the lakes are connected by small streams (Delias Run is the main one). Delias Run feeds into Indian River, an excellent canoe route outside the area. Northern pike, largemouth and smallmouth bass, perch and bluegill provide excellent year-around fishing. Neds Lake contains eastern brook trout.

Wildlife in the area includes ruffed grouse, woodcock, beaver, pine squirrel, otter, red fox, white-tailed deer, coyote, black bear, and

17

moose. Greater sandhill crane, loon, bald eagle, and osprey visit the area. Timber and plant growth in the area includes aspen-paper birch, sugar maple, red maple, beech, red, white and jack pine, white cedar, spruce, balsam fir, and tamarack.

Temperatures average from the mid-60s in the summer to 20 below in the winter, but it can get even colder, a matter to be considered if hiking or backpacking the area during the winter season. Precipitation averages about 34 inches annually. Average snow depth is about 48 inches, making this excellent country for cross-country skiing and snowshoeing from late November to mid-April.

To reach the area: From Munising, drive northwest on M-94, a primary state highway which passes just one and a half miles east of the wilderness. Take county gravel road #437 to the area.

WHERE TO DRIVE

The entire area around the wilderness strongly resembles its character, so driving along M-94 does give the motorist some idea of what this countryside is like. County Roads #437 which bounds the wilderness on the south and 445 on the west also provide excellent drives to experience the terrain and if you'll keep a sharp eye, you may see some of the wildlife which inhabits this area.

WHERE TO HIKE

Some 20 miles of roads and seven miles of old logging railroad grades traverse the area, all of which are used as hiking trails. Also a portage trail connecting several of the lakes also can be used as a hiking trail. Since canoeing is popular in this area, the trail will be primarily maintained by the Forest Service for canoeists. Otherwise, hikers are invited to find their own way through the woodland.

BACKPACKING OPPORTUNITIES

Although established trails are limited in this area, backpackers are welcome. Primitive camping is permitted throughout the area as long as it creates no abuse problems. The soils are fragile here,

however, and backpackers are urged to take special care not to abuse the terrain or its plant and animal inhabitants. Usable water is available from streams and lakes throughout the area. Be sure to take along a good insect repellent, however, and in some seasons—particularly spring and early summer—mosquito veiling may be necessary.

WHERE TO CAMP

Primitive camping is permitted throughout the area, but campers are urged to be particularly careful with fire. The use of stoves is urged wherever possible in order to avoid fire dangers. Preferred camping spots, of course, are on lakes and streams, but you may choose your own. For winter camping, check with the Forest Service before going into the area.

Where to Obtain Information

Forest Supervisor
Hiawatha Nat'l Forest
Escanaba, MI 49829

isle royale national park

AT ISLE ROYALE National Park is a sign prologue which reads: "Enchantment is here: Nature in all her moods of peace and violence, an island of mystery and scientific exploration, the world's largest freshwater lake, and the site of 4,000 years of human history. Take time to savor all these things; you will be well rewarded." The largest island in Lake Superior, Isle Royale is some 45 miles long and nine miles across at its widest point, occupying some 210 square miles. It may well be the truest example of wilderness in Mid-America for no vehicles are allowed here. To get there, you must either go by boat or float plane, and to get around the island, you must hike.

The complex is an archipelago of more than 200 small islands and countless minor rocks protruding from the waters of Superior. Highest point on the main island is Mount Desor, 792 feet above lake level. The solitude provided here will be long remembered. The island is the creation of volcanoes, the Great Glacier, and water. The island is a series of eroded valleys extending its full length between rock beds of hard baslat such as the massive Greenstone Ridge, which forms the backbone of the island.

Forests dominate the island scenery with red maple, sugar maple, yellow birch, bigtooth aspen, northern red oak, and white pine. Coniferous evergreens include white spruce and balsam fir, white birch, quaking aspen, mountain ash, and jack pine.

Since the island is only 15 miles from Canadian shores, some of the wildlife found here crosses on the ice during winter. Among that seen is beaver, muskrat, mink, weasel, red squirrel, snowshoe hare, moose, and wolf. In fact, here are located the most extensive wolf packs in the lower 48 states. More than 200 species of birds including the pileated woodpecker, bald eagle, osprey, and some 25 types of warblers are found here in addition to the most common bird—the herring gull.

Before you visit the island, make sure to pack plenty of warm clothing and a first-aid kit. Nights are cool and a doctor is many miles away by water. There are no poisonous snakes or poisonous-to-touch plants here, however.

To reach Isle Royale: Take US 41 to Houghton, where you can obtain ferry or charter float plane service to the island. In Minnesota, take US 61 to Grand Portage along the north shore of Lake Superior which also offers boat and plane service to the island during summer months. The island is not normally open to the public except by special permit during winter.

WHERE TO DRIVE

No motor vehicles are permitted on the island.

WHERE TO HIKE

A complex of hiking trails extends throughout the island, providing the hiker a superlative experience in the wilderness. A single trail leads along the crest of Greenstone Ridge from one end of the island to the other, a distance of about 40 miles. A large loop trail leads off this main trail past Feldtman Lake and along Feldtman Ridge to Siskiwit Bay, then back west again to join the Greenstone Trail.

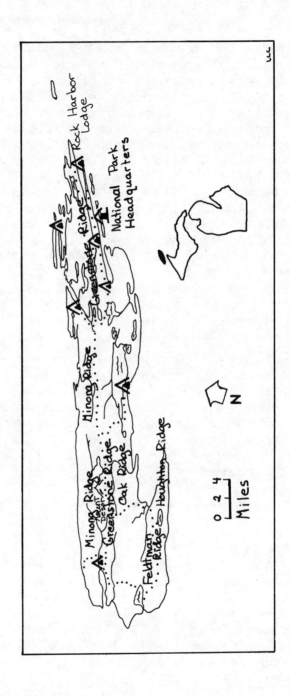

Minong Ridge

Minong Ridge

Greenstone Ridge
Mount
Desor

Oak Ridge

Greenstone Ridge

Feldtman
Ridge

Houghton Ridge

National Park
Headquarters

Rock Harbor
Lodge

N

0 2 4
Miles

Typical scene—interior of Isle Royale in Michigan

Other trails lead off at Lake LaSage, Ishpeming Point, Hatchet Lake, McCargo Cove, Moskey Basin, and Daisy Farm. Another loop trail follows the lakefront to Rock Harbor Lodge.

BACKPACKING OPPORTUNITIES

Backpacking is excellent. With a variety of established campsites and plenty of water suitable for use (you might want to purify it by either boiling or treating with chemicals), backpackers will find this place most to their liking. There's an abundance of firewood, but again, backpackers are asked to use stoves whenever possible and conserve the wood. Be sure to bring along plenty of insect repellent—black flies and mosquitoes are dedicated residents of the islands and resent intruders.

WHERE TO CAMP

Camping here is most delightful. The solitude of wilderness trails and vistas of wave-swept shores will not soon be forgotten. Several established campgrounds are located on the island, some of them suitable for boat camping. Since there are no regularly operated grocery stores campers should bring most provisions with them. Limited supplies are available at Rock Harbor Lodge. Be sure to bring warm clothing since the nights become very cool.

Maps are available showing the trail system from the park headquarters or Visitor Center. If you bring stoves, you must purchase your fuel at one of the lodges on the island. None can be carried aboard commercial charter boat. Fog is common during June and early July. Lake storms are prevalent in early September. A camper's boat service is provided by Rock Harbor Lodge to Daisy Farm, Mosky Basin, Tobin Harbor, and other more distant points. Rates vary with distance and number of persons. Excursions and trolling fishing trips are available at Rock Harbor Lodge and Windigo Inn.

Where to Obtain Information

Park Superintendent
Isle Royale Nat'l Park
Houghton, MI 49931

National Park Concessions, Inc.
Mammoth Cave, KY 42259

rock river canyon

CONTAINING SOME 5,380 acres in the Hiawatha National Forest on Michigan's Upper Peninsula just a short distance from Lake Superior, once logged Rock River Canyon is now being reclaimed by nature. This is a rugged canyon area with sheer sandstone bluffs and numerous overlooks offering a view of the canyon over the tops of giant pine and hemlock. Rock River Falls, combined with several other intermittent waterfalls and excellent water quality, add to the attractiveness of the area.

The climate here is as rugged as the walls of the canyon, however, and highly changeable. It's possible to have snow into early June and again in early September. Insects normally are a problem all through the summer—particularly in June—and if you visit, be sure to bring along veils and plenty of insect repellent for protection against black flies, mosquitoes, and deer flies. Days are warm during the summer, but nights generally are cool enough for a sweater. Fishing is excellent for trout..

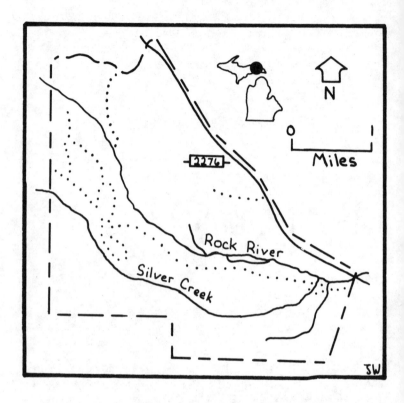

To reach the area: From Chatham, take FS Road 2279 north. It borders the eastern boundary of the area.

WHERE TO DRIVE

To appreciate the area fully, one must hike into it. But there are some FS roads which allow one to see the fringes without getting into the heart. FS Road 2279 borders the eastern boundary; FS Road 2276 borders the northern side. A dirt road leads off FS Road 2276 to the vicinity of Rock Canyon Falls where you can hike a short distance to the falls.

WHERE TO HIKE

An old logging trail leads through the area south of the river extending some five miles east to west. One may enter the trail from FS Road 2278 in the vicinity of Spider Ponds and hike it along the stream past the falls to a point where it connects up with Road E-39 north of Rumely.

BACKPACKING OPPORTUNITIES

This is excellent backpacking territory, although no established camping areas are available along the way. Water from the stream is pure enough to drink or use for cooking. Beware of black bear and store your food accordingly.

WHERE TO CAMP

Choose your own campsite, but make sure to leave no signs of it once you've left the area. If you wish to use an established campground, a Forest Service campground with 19 sites is located just a couple of miles east of the area at Au Train Lake. Also boating, fishing, swimming and well water are available here.

Where to Obtain Information

District Ranger
U.S. Forest Service
Munising, MI 49862

Forest Supervisor
Hiawatha Nat'l Forest
Escanaba, MI 49829

seney wilderness

IN THE CENTER of Michigan's Upper Peninsula is a most unique bog area called the Seney Wilderness, a part of the Seney National Wildlife Refuge. Comprising some 25,150 acres, it represents one of the southernmost-patterned string bogs in the lower 48 states. In fact, only in recent years were such bogs recognized in the Great Lakes area. The patterned terrain of this area is a complex of bogs and fens. As with most patterned ground, the better examples can be reached only on foot, or by a combination of canoe and foot travel. In this case, canoes aren't practical, so one must walk in order to experience the area. And because of horrendous black flies and mosquitoes, it's best to do it in either the winter or late September to mid-November.

The climate normally is as rugged as the terrain and snows can occur as early as September and as late as May. Extreme temperatures sometimes occur—as low as 47 degrees below zero and up to 100 or more in the summer. Average precipitation is about 31 inches. Winds are particularly strong in the spring and fall.

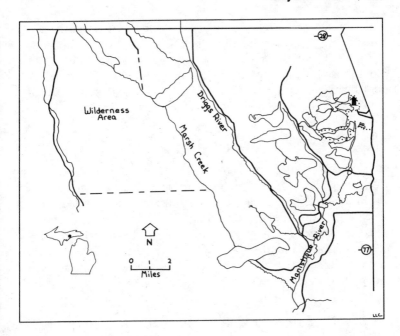

The most numerous species of wildlife found in this area are ruffed grouse, herring gull, snowshoe hare, whitefoot mouse, raven, and white-tailed deer. Occasionally black bear and bobcat are seen along with coyote, timber wolf, otter, mink, moose, bald eagle, and osprey.

The bog islands are commonly dominated by a few red pine with some jack pine or aspen. They are usually fringed with thick clumps of alder and in some locations long stands of tamarack. Black spruce swamps are found along the edges of the bog while thin stands of aspen or jack pine with numerous shrubs share the burned over uplands with large charred pine stumps.

To reach the Refuge: From I-75 south of Sault Ste. Marie, take M-28 west to the town of Seney, then south five miles on M-77 to the refuge entrance road.

WHERE TO DRIVE

M-28 parallels the northern boundary of the refuge; M-77 along the eastern boundary. The Manistique River runs from near Germfask through a portion of the refuge and is an excellent canoe stream. No access is allowed in the refuge, however, one may float through it and observe and photograph wildlife enroute. That doesn't come close to the wilderness area, but it's certainly a worthwhile experience to combine with a driving tour. A self-guided auto tour has been established near the refuge headquarters.

WHERE TO HIKE

No hiking trails have been established in the area, although visitors are permitted to hike into the wilderness area from August 1st to March 15, finding their own way in and out. Off-road vehicles such as snowmobiles and dune buggies are not permitted anywhere on the refuge. It's a good idea to use a topographic map and compass for this journey. Be sure to take plenty of insect repellent as well as drinking water. Also near the headquarters is a short loop nature trail worth taking.

BACKPACKING OPPORTUNITIES

Backpacking is permitted in the wilderness area from August 1st to March 15, but no overnight camping is allowed on the refuge. Two small creeks—Luce and Marsh Creek—flow through the northern part of the bog area.

WHERE TO CAMP

No camping is permitted on the refuge, but there are private campgrounds in the general area. For locations and specific data, contact the Dept. of Natural Resources office at Newberry.

Where to Obtain Information

Refuge Manager
Seney Wildlife Refuge
Seney, MI 49883

DNR District Office
Newberry, MI 49868

sleeping bear dune

ALONG LAKE MICHIGAN on Michigan's Upper Peninsula is Sleeping Bear Dune, a national lakeshore under the administration of the National Park Service. It includes some 60,000 acres, including South and North Manitou islands in Lake Michigan. It was only established in 1970. Presently, much of the land with the exception of South Manitou Island is privately owned, for the park will be under development for many years. Meanwhile, it is open to some limited public use.

Your visit should begin with a stop at the visitor contact station for information and exhibits telling the geological and maritime story of this region. The park plans call for inclusion of 30 miles of Lake Michigan shore with a special 30-mile scenic parkway running north and south from Little Traverse Lake to Honor. The lakeshore includes a variety of landforms—dunes, ridges, valleys, plains, streams, and lakes. The sand dune desert provides striking contrast to the hardwood forests.

Sleeping Bear Dunes National Lakeshore, Michigan, is noted for its beaches, massive sand dunes, forests, and lakes.

In fall, this is a popular area with the glowing colors of beech and basswood, oaks, red maples, and large stands of chalk-white birches. Ghost forests where the moving sand dunes have devoured parts of the trees are evident at many places. On South Manitou Island is a special attraction—the Valley of Giants, a remnant of the region's virgin forests. Here are tall white cedars, many of them more than 500 years old, common and redberry elder, mountain and sugar maple, white ash, and basswood.

Throughout the lakeshore, you'll find an abundance of wildlife including porcupine, white-tailed deer, bobcat, and more than 220 species of birds. Loons nest in the small marshy ponds near the Platte River and there also are numerous species of ducks, Canada geese and snow geese, long-legged blue herons, and an occasional sandhill crane. Atop the wind-swept and sandy plateaus one finds the domain of vesper sparrow, horned lark, and goldfinch.

Fishing is good to excellent for rock bass, bluegill, and northern

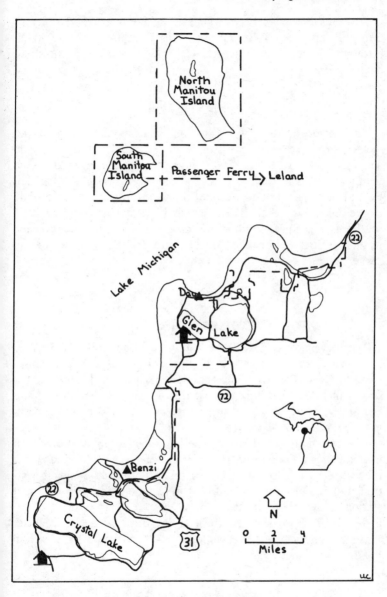

pike in the lakes. Coho salmon run on the Platte, providing early autumn fishing excitement.

To reach the area: From Manistee, take either US 31 north to Benzonia and turn west on M-115 to Frankfort or take M-22 through Elberta to Frankfort where is located the lakeshore headquarters.

WHERE TO DRIVE

The major portion of the national lakeshore runs from the vicinity of Crystal Lake west of Honor to a point north of Little Traverse Lake. M-22 generally runs through the lakeshore area with spur roads leading westward to the shores of Lake Michigan. Best place to get closeup views of the dunes from your automobile is the D.H. Day State Park, which is also within the national seashore area. Since much of the property is still privately owned at this writing, visitors are asked to respect the rights of property owners and stay out of those areas.

WHERE TO HIKE

The best places to hike and climb the sand dunes is at D.H. Day State Park just north of the Visitor Contact Station and Great Sleeping Bear Dune or at Benzi State Park near Mud Lake. Otherwise, only limited hiking experiences are now provided, but the Park Service suggests that will change as more and more property is added to the lakeshore area.

The best hiking wilderness experience can be enjoyed on South Manitou Island, which comprises 5,000 acres. Old trail roads on the island permit excellent hiking opportunities. A ranger is stationed there during the period May to October. The visitor contact station or lakeshore headquarters can provide recommendations and detailed maps showing those trails. But to get to the island, you must go by boat. A passenger ferry service is operated from the town of Leland to the island during the summer months.

BACKPACKING OPPORTUNITIES

The greatest backpacking opportunities are on South Manitou Island where one can escape the crowds (except on summer weekends) and commune with nature. Water is available and most of the island is heavily vegetated with good trails for hiking. Again, insect repellent is a must during the warm months.

WHERE TO CAMP

Primitive camping is permitted on South Manitou Island, but as it becomes more popular, the Park Service forsees limiting it to a specified number because of heavy use. Some campers also have abused the area with littering, cutting, etc. Camping also is available on the mainland in the state parks at established campgrounds. On South Manitou, campers are urged to use cookstoves and limit their use of the island's firewood.

Where to Obtain Information

Superintendent
Sleeping Bear Dune Nat'l Lakeshore
400 Main St.
Frankfort, MI 49635

sylvania tract

AT THE WESTERN end of Michigan's Upper Peninsula lies Sylvania, labeled a Recreation Area of the Ottawa National Forest. But, in essence, it is a veritable wilderness totally capable of providing a most unique wilderness experience. With 21,000 acres—4,000 of which are in water so clear and clean you can drink it direct from the lake, Sylvania is a combination of bog, muskeg, virgin forest, lakes, and small streams. The forests here are hemlock, maple, birch, and associated species of northern hardwoods.

With 36 named lakes and countless others, Sylvania offers great canoeing and fishing opportunities for largemouth, smallmouth bass, northern pike, and walleye as well as lake trout. Only two lakes allow motors—Crooked and Long Lakes, and those are close to main roads leading into the area. Wildlife includes porcupine, white-tailed deer, black bear, badger, raccoon, and a multitude of others.

(U.S. Forest Service)

Fishing at the south end of Deer Island Lake in the Sylvania Recreation Area, Ottawa National Forest, Michigan

Climate is rugged and one may encounter snow in late May and as early as mid-September. Snowfall in winter may exceed 140 inches accumulation, with temperatures 30 below zero.

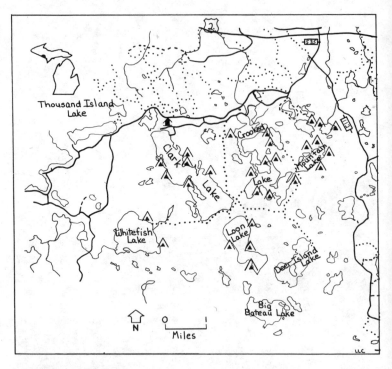

To reach the area: From Iron River, take US 2 west to Watersmeet, headquarters for the District U.S. Forest Ranger where you may obtain information. Proceed then to CR 535 south which will lead you directly into the Sylvania Recreation Area.

WHERE TO DRIVE

CR 535 takes the motorist through some scenic portions of Sylvania. At Long Lake a Forest Service Road bears left past Whitefish Lake and into Wisconsin. These two roads, however, give motorists an excellent opportunity to view portions of the area and become somewhat acquainted with it.

WHERE TO HIKE

This is excellent hiking country. The trails are gentle and soft from an old forest. Trails lead throughout the area, giving one the opportunity to explore most of the lakes without benefit of a canoe. Canoeing is a great sport, however, and if combined with hiking can provide double fun. Insects are bothersome all summer long, generally—mosquitoes, black flies, and deer flies.

BACKPACKING OPPORTUNITIES

Since many campsites are designated in this area, it makes for ideal backpacking. You don't even have to worry about finding a place, for backpackers must obtain a permit before entering the area. This way the number of people using the area at any one time is controlled.

WHERE TO CAMP

There are 29 wilderness campgrounds having a total of 84 family units, each with a table, tent pad, fire ring, and vault toilet. You must bring your own water, however, or use that from the lakes only after chemically treating or boiling. All camping is primitive. Those using campers will find other established campgrounds nearby in the Ottawa National Forest.

All visitors to Sylvania are required to register before entering the area. In addition all backpackers and campers must camp at campsites previously registered and requested.

Where to Obtain Information

Forest Supervisor
Ottawa Nat'l Forest
Ironwood, MI 49938

District Ranger
U.S. Forest Service
Watersmeet, MI 49969

WISCONSIN

blackjack springs wilderness

IN FAMOUS VILAS County in Wisconsin's Nicolet National Forest only a few miles west as a crow flies of Whisker Lake Wilderness is Blackjack Springs Wilderness. Like Whisker, it is small, but impressive. Consisting of 2,560 acres, it contains essentially the same terrain, vegetative and wildlife characteristics as Whisker Lake and Sylvania across the border on Michigan's Upper Peninsula.

Because of that similarity, we need not go into detail here but instead refer the reader to the next section on Whisker Lake Wilderness. The area contains much of the drainage of Blackjack Creek, an excellent trout stream. No lakes of any size are found here, although there are several wildlife watering holes.

To reach the area: From SR 70 east of Eagle River, take Forest Service Road 2178 (the old military road) north along the northeastern boundary.

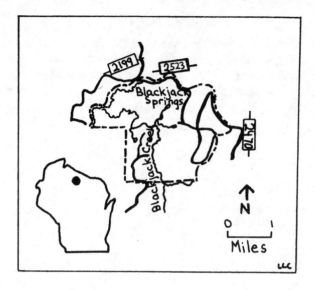

WHERE TO DRIVE

Besides FS Road 2178, one may tour the northern boundary of the wilderness via FS Road 2523 or drive close to the western boundary via FS Road 2199. All these are dirt roads and may be driven only from May to early October.

WHERE TO HIKE

No trails exist here, although you may hike along some FS roads in the area. If the area is designated wilderness, these will be closed to all automotive traffic and will revert entirely to hiking trails. The terrain is generally open enough, however, that you may find your own way through the wilderness.

BACKPACKING OPPORTUNITIES

Backpackers are welcome. Find your own site; best ones are along the creek drainage. Refer to Whisker Lake section for other details.

WHERE TO CAMP

No established campsites have been provided within the wilderness; make your own, but be careful to leave only footprints. Several Forest Service campgrounds are located close to the area, however, including Spectacle Lake to the northeast, Kentuck Lake to the east, and Anvil Lake to the southeast. All have drinking water and pit toilets.

Where to Obtain Information

Forest Supervisor
Nicolet Nat'l Forest
Rhinelander, WI 54501

rainbow lake wilderness

IN THE NORTHERN part of Wisconsin's Chequamegon National Forest is a fascinating 6,583-acre chunk of wilderness called Rainbow Lake. It's an outstanding example, first of all, of a northern hardwood forest and rolling glaciated lake country. It has many outstanding primitive bodies of water; here one can enjoy a northern Wisconsin wilderness-type experience without intrusions or activities associated with man. There are 15 undeveloped lakes five acres or larger in size and nine ponds of less than five acres. All are landlocked and there are no streams within the wilderness.

The area acquired its name from one of those lakes in the central part of the area—one at which rainbows were often seen. Vegetation includes white birch, aspen, maple, and a number of other hardwood types. The area is particularly beautiful in late September-early October during the peak of autumn color.

Wildlife in the area includes deer, black bear, otter, mink, cottontail rabbit, opossum, raccoon, skunk, badger, fox and squirrels,

43

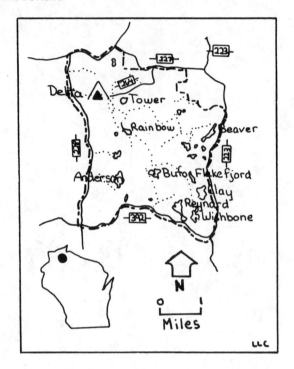

owls, and numerous species of woodpeckers. Walleyes, northern pike, and lake trout are found in these lakes. Anderson, Beaver and Reynard lakes are particularly good for fishing. Climate offers potential year-around use. Although temperatures sometimes drop to 30 or 40 degrees below zero and rise to 90 in the summer, the variety of activities available make it a year-around use area.

Snowshoeing and cross-country skiing are popular in winter as well as winter camping, backpacking and ice fishing. Annual precipitation is about 30 inches with most of it coming during the summer months. Snow normally starts to accumulate in mid-November and reaches a depth of 24 to 36 inches.

To reach the area: From Delta, take Forest Service Road 223 south to FS Road 227 (west), one-half mile to the northeast corner of the area. From Drummond, take Forest Service Road 223 north to Forest Road 392 and the southeast corner of the area.

WHERE TO DRIVE

Roads bound all sides of this particular wilderness, making it ideal to visit by automobile. On the south is FS Road 392, on the east FS Road 223, on the north 227 and 228, the latter running along the western boundary as well. While the timber stands are dense, the drive along these roads during the early morning and late afternoon likely will afford the motorist the opportunity to view some of the wildlife of the area as well as to gain a feel for this particular wilderness.

WHERE TO HIKE

While visitors to the area may make their own way through this wilderness, particularly in late fall, winter or early spring when the vegetation is less dense, there are old logging trails which wind through the area, some connecting with the lakes. These are generally easy trails to hike. They are not marked. A few of the trails have been traveled enough so the hiker would have little difficulty. However, he should use a topographic map and compass just to be on the safe side. These add dimension to any outdoor adventure in the wilderness anyway. A single cross-country trail leading directly across the wilderness extends from the southeastern corner near Wishbone Lake diagonally past Rainbow Lake, Bufo Lake, Tower Lake, Raynard Lake, and leaves the wilderness at the northwestern corner.

BACKPACKING OPPORTUNITIES

The entire area is good for backpacking. Lake water is of high quality. As with any water, precaution should be taken to purify it before drinking. And the lakes are so situated one need not carry a great supply of drinking water during his backpacking adventure if he is prepared to purify his own. During the summer and spring months, take along a good insect repellent for both mosquitoes, black flies, and deer flies can present a problem, as well as no-see-ums.

WHERE TO CAMP

No camping is permitted. The US Forest Service also has an established campground—Perch Lake—with 16 sites, drinking water, and pit toilets just outside the wilderness on the east. A private campground is also located just west of Delta on Lake Delta. A number of other campgrounds, both Forest Service and private, are located within a 30-mile radius of the area.

Where to Obtain Information

Forest Supervisor
Chequamegon Nat'l Forest
Park Falls, WI 54552

whisker lake wilderness

ALONG THE SOUTH banks of the Brule River which divides Michigan's pristine Upper Peninsula country from Wisconsin lies the Whisker Lake Wilderness, comprising 2,735 acres in the Nicolet National Forest. In character it is similar to some of the wilderness or semi-wilderness areas of the UP—Sylvania, the McCormick Tract and others. For here are great hemlocks, white cedar in the boggy sections, birch, tamarack, red maple, aspen, and a multitude of other plantlife.

Running from Whisker Lake, located near the center of the wilderness, is the Riley Creek drainage, a beautiful high-quality trout stream with water suitable for drinking. It flows through a cathedral garden of northern woodland where one is likely to spot white-tailed deer, black bear, badger, mink, otter, fox, and many other residents of the wild kingdom. Bald eagles have been spotted here, but because of heavy vegetation the area is not considered prime bird watching territory. Rainbow and brook trout are found in the stream.

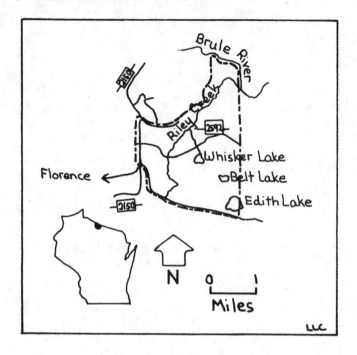

Besides Whisker, two other lakes—Bell and Edith—are located in this wilderness. They provide some largemouth bass, brook, and rainbow trout fishing.

To reach the area: From Florence, take SR 70 west to Forest Service Road 2150 (north) which leads along the western boundary of the wilderness.

WHERE TO DRIVE

This is excellent wilderness to explore by automobile. Forest Service Road 2151 extends along the southern boundary. It's a dirt road, but certainly provides a worthwhile drive during the months of May to early October. The western boundary is formed by FS Road 2150 which also provides an excellent opportunity to sample the area. Drive these roads slowly just at dusk or early in the morning for the best opportunities to view the wildlife, particularly grazing white-tailed deer.

WHERE TO HIKE

Hiking trails are not plentiful in this wilderness, but the terrain (gently rolling) and vegetation make it possible to explore your own way through much of the area. A Forest Service road extending through the midsection of the wilderness makes an excellent hiking trail and there's another (a six-mile hunter's trace) which leads generally along Riley Creek. This is a small patch of wilderness that can be experienced in a day or two, depending upon how much detail you wish to study.

BACKPACKING OPPORTUNITIES

Backpackers are welcome and many like to camp around one of the lakes or along the stream. Insects can be a problem during the summer months, particularly mosquitoes, black flies, and deer flies. Take along a good repellent and perhaps you'll want to consider face netting as well. Since the nights here are cool even during summer, it's also best to pack some warm clothing. Snows sometimes come as late as May and as early as September, but they usually appear only as flurries. Snow accumulates to depths of four feet in winter.

WHERE TO CAMP

Choose your own campsite. Near the water is best for the convenience of having it close by. No established sites are located in the area, but there are some within a short driving distance in the Nicolet National Forest. For locations, consult the Forest Ranger Station at Florence.

Where to Obtain Information

District Ranger
U.S. Forest Service
Florence, WI 54121

Forest Supervisor
Nicolet Nat'l Forest
Rhinelander, WI 54501

MINNESOTA

agassiz wilderness

JUST FORTY MILES from the Canadian border in northwest Minnesota is the Agassiz National Wildlife Refuge, occupying a small inlet bay of glacial Lake Agassiz. In the center of this 61,487-acre refuge is a veritable northern wilderness comprising 4,000 acres. It's a fantastic northern forest and bog area including natural lakes, pristine streams, and an abundance of wildlife including a number of large animals.

Because the area is so level, it is poorly drained and extensive marshes exist throughout the area. The watershed here empties into the Red Lake River and then the north-flowing Red River of the North, which empties ultimately into Hudson Bay. Elevations in this wilderness are relatively constant near 1,140 feet above sea level. Two small lakes are located in the wilderness area—Kuriko, about 50 acres in size, and Whiskey Lake, comprising some 20 acres. Neither have any fish life.

Dense stands of black spruce-tamarack cover the area. Other

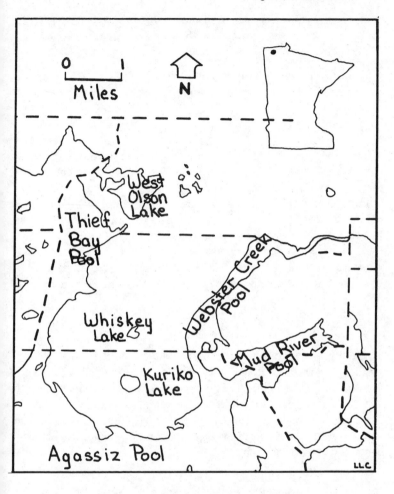

Miles

N

West Olson Lake

Thief Bay Pool

Webster Creek Pool

Whiskey Lake

Mud River Pool

Kuriko Lake

Agassiz Pool

LLC

vegetation includes willow and aspen, along with many bog-type plants. Although many migrating waterfowl use the area, moose are the key attraction. More than 250 are believed to occupy the refuge, many of them in the wilderness area. Also here are elk, coyote, bobcat, black bear, red fox, badger, river otter, mink, fisher, woodchuck, porcupine, muskrat, beaver, snowshoe hare, and occasionally a timber wolf is seen. White-tailed deer are abundant.

More than 250 species of birds are found, including five species of grebes which nest here. Temperatures in winter can be very cold, ranging down to nearly 50 below zero to more than 100 in summer. Insects—mosquitoes and black flies—are often a problem in the spring and early summer months.

To reach the refuge: From Thief River Falls and US 59 take SR 32 north to Holt, then turn right and follow refuge signs.

WHERE TO DRIVE

This countryside is an interesting drive. Several wildlife management areas—Thief Lake, Eckvall and Elm lakes—are located near the area and you might wish to drive past them just to see the wildlife. But you also may drive through the refuge from Holt on a county road or on seasonal refuge roads leading from the refuge headquarters to various points. Check with the refuge manager first, however, to determine just where to drive. Certain areas are closed at certain times of the year in the interest of protecting wildlife. There is a self-guided auto drive through the refuge. Ask about it.

WHERE TO HIKE

Hiking is only authorized by first contacting the Refuge Manager. Hiking trails, per se, have not been developed because of limited funds and demand. The area provides good opportunity to see wildlife providing hikers are quiet and use stealth in approaching areas likely to be inhabited by wildlife. Be careful of moose—keep your distance—for they may charge, particularly when the cows have young.

BACKPACKING OPPORTUNITIES

No backpacking is permitted because of the primary objective of the refuge—the preservation of habitat for wildlife. Overnight use is not encouraged.

WHERE TO CAMP

No campgrounds have been established on the refuge and there's no camping in the area, except for one primitive site available near the refuge boundary. There is camping less than an hour's drive away at two state parks, however, Lake Bronson, near the town of Lake Bronson on US 59, and Old Mill, just west of US 59 near New Folden. No overnight camping is permitted on the refuge.

Where to Obtain Information

Refuge Manager
Agassiz Nat'l Wildlife Refuge
Middle River, MN 56737

boundary waters canoe area

ASTRIDE THE MINNESOTA-Canadian border and extending
200 miles northwest from Lake Superior is an extravagant land of
forests and waters unique on this continent—the Boundary Waters
Canoe Area—a veritable wilderness dotted with thousands of tiny
islands. Fashioned from ancient mountains, this rugged terrain with
thousands of glacier lakes connected by short blue rivers and
streams, is actually within the Superior National Forest and administered by the U.S. Forest Service. And although here, too, man once
made his imprint, today's canoeists travel its ancient waterways in
the same setting as Indians and French *voyageurs* did long ago. Here
they find solitude, adventure, and freedom in a wild land of shining
lakes, sparkling rivers and rocky pine-clad shores.

Its preservation is not new; it was set aside in 1926 as a roadless
area to preserve its primitive character. It consists of more than one
million acres of land and water. There are more than 1,200 miles of
canoe trail. The entire BWCA is underlain with the oldest rocks on

Scene in the Boundary Waters Canoe Area, northeastern Minnesota

the continent and some of the most spectacular shorelines are formed by their vertical rock faces.

Principal vegetation here are pines—jack, white, and red—but there are also white and black spruce, balsam fir, northern white cedar and tamarack, as well as quaking aspen, paper birch and, occasionally, maple. A great variety of wild flowers including some sub-arctic species can be found here.

Wildlife includes substantial populations of timber wolves, fisher, white-tailed deer, moose, black bear, otter, weasel, mink, coyote, muskrat, beaver, fox, and a variety of squirrels. Fish include walleye, northern pike, and lake trout. Some of the lakes have small-mouth bass, bluegill and crappie, as well as rainbow and brook trout.

To reach the area: Although there are several points of entry, the two most popular ones seem to be Ely and Grand Marais. To get to the latter from Duluth, take US 61 north where are outfitters to direct you to the Gunflint Trail. At the head of this you'll find

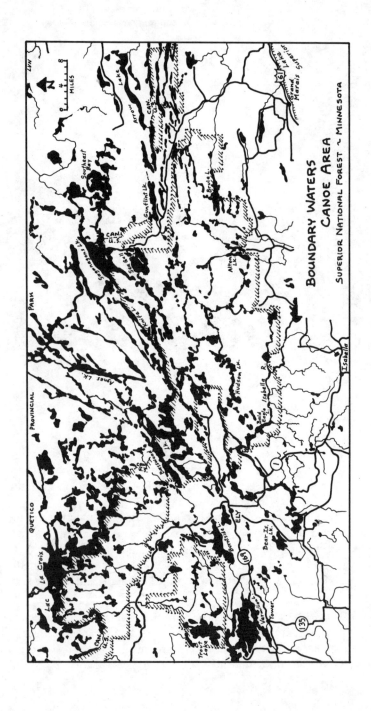

BOUNDARY WATERS
CANOE AREA

SUPERIOR NATIONAL FOREST ～ MINNESOTA

yourself launched upon a most remarkable canoeing adventure. To reach Ely, take US north to SR 1 which leads to Ely.

WHERE TO DRIVE

Several roads, most of them dirt, lead through the vicinity of the BWCA and the motorist can actually enjoy a most worthwhile drive during the warm months. From Ely, the Echo Trail leads northwest for many miles with spur Forest Service roads leading off it at various points. Take any of them. They all lead to some spectacular scenery and the opportunity to chance across wildlife. Also from Ely is the Fernberg Road leading northeast.

The Gunflint Trail from Grand Marais leads some 68 miles into canoe country. All these roads lead through territory which appears as wild as the day the *voyageurs* first discovered this land.

WHERE TO HIKE

A great number of hiking and portage trails have been established in the area. One of the finest hiking trails is Forest Service Trail 147 which leads for miles through the eastern portion of the lake country, extending from the Fernberg Road northeast of Ely to the Gunflint Trail. For detailed maps, guides, tips and recommendations, contact the U.S. Forest Service. It's good to take a topographic map—and make sure you know how to read it—as well as a compass before hiking here.

BACKPACKING OPPORTUNITIES

You may backpack any of the trails in the Boundary Waters, or take out cross-country. Make sure you know where you're going, however, or else you may end up with wet feet. A topo map and compass are indispensable here; so is a good insect repellent for mosquitoes, black flies and deer flies can be a major nuisance. Thunderstorms during the summer months are sometimes violent. Remember to stay away from tall trees and be sure to pack rain gear.

WHERE TO CANOE

It would take an entire book to describe the many many canoe trails in the BWCA. Unless you hire a guide—and though many are available during the summer months, you should make reservations well in advance—you'll need to make sure you're proficient at reading a topo map and compass and mark off the landmarks as you canoe past them. Otherwise you may become the object of a search party—and the rangers dislike those.

WHERE TO CAMP

Campsites are marked on most of the maps issued by outfitters in the area and the Forest Service urges you to use existing sites since the area is so heavily used anyway. Also, several established Forest Service campgrounds are located on roads whereby you may drive to them. Six are located along the Gunflint Trail, one, a private facility, is virtually in Grand Marais. Other private campgrounds are nearby also.

Where to Obtain Information

Forest Supervisor
Superior Nat'l Forest
Box 338
Duluth, MN 55801

Minnesota Dept. of Natural Resources
Centennial Bldg.
St. Paul, MN 55101

mille lacs
and rice lake wilderness

THIS WILDERNESS COMPRISES 1,400 acres of Minnesota bog and an island in Rice Lake (6.27 acres in size) as well as two small boulder islands—Spirit and Hennepin, both measuring under an acre in size—in Mille Lacs Lake. It is a part of the Rice Lake and Mille Lacs Islands National Wildlife Refuges, comprising some 18,056 acres in central Minnesota. In fact, the refuges lie within the transition zone between Minnesota's coniferous and hardwood forests. And, of course, the major portion of activity is around Rice Lake, 3,800 acres in size, with its famous beds of wild rice.

It's a glaciated area, a system of moraines or glacial ridges in the shape of a huge horseshoe. Mille Lacs Lake lies inside the bottom of the horseshoe and is a classic example of a moraine-dammed lake. Spirit and Hennepin Islands are a mix of glacial boulders, sand and gravel pushed up by ice action and since weathered by wind and waves. The mainland wilderness is essentially a northern bog used primarily by wildlife.

59

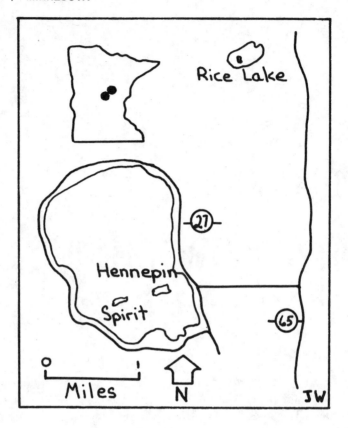

In this area one finds many species of waterfowl, both ducks and geese, as well as bald and gold eagles, osprey, pileated wood-peckers, greater sandhill cranes, the peregrine falcon, common loon, sharp-tailed grouse, and upland plover. There are also black bear, moose, white-tailed deer, timber wolf, mink, muskrat, beaver, otter, porcupine, badger, weasel, and several species of squirrels.

Northern pike and bullheads predominate in the fish populations, but there also are walleye, yellow perch, buffalo, and eelpout. Temperatures range from 40 below zero during winters to the high 90s during summers. Snow cover is assured during winter, making it an ideal place to cross-country ski or snowshoe.

To reach the area: The Rice Lake Wilderness area is some 16 miles northeast of Mille Lacs Lake. From the Twin Cities to Mille Lacs Lake, consult a road map for the best route as there are several, the choice depending on which side of the lake one wishes to visit. A popular route to the south shore is #169 north from Elk River. From Duluth, take I-35 southwest to SR 27 at Moose Lake. Turn west to SR 65, then north only a short distance to the Rice Lake National Wildlife Refuge headquarters.

WHERE TO DRIVE

At Mille Lacs Lake, vying with the Red Lake reservoirs as the largest bodies of water in the state, highways 169, 18 and 47 loop around the lake giving the motorist an opportunity to view the entire area. The only way, of course, to reach the two tiny wilderness islands is by boat and that may or may not be possible. They are visited primarily by fishermen and bird watchers, but during windy weather, the boulder-strewn shores are almost unapproachable because of hazardous conditions. They are excellent nesting places for gulls and terns.

There are roads in the vicinity of the wilderness at Rice Lake, but since they may be closed at certain periods of the year to avoid disturbing wildlife, it's best to check with the refuge manager before planning your visit.

WHERE TO HIKE

A number of dirt patrol roads lead through the refuge area and these are excellent for hiking. Since they may at times be closed to the public, be sure to check with the refuge manager in advance of a visit. No specified hiking trails exist in the refuge. On Rice Lake Island, one may hike around the island, but no trails exist here either, although the vegetation, itself, is not dense enough to discourage the hiker. But one must get to the island by boat or canoe.

BACKPACKING OPPORTUNITIES

Although backpacking is not specifically forbidden, no overnight camping is permitted in the refuge area mainly because it likely would disturb the wildlife.

WHERE TO CAMP

No camping areas exist on the refuge and none are planned. Even primitive camping is forbidden since the refuge is not geared for overnight use. Camping areas do exist in the vicinity, however; check with refuge personnel for their recommendations.

Where to Obtain Information

Refuge Manager
Rice Lake Nat'l Wildlife Refuge
McGregor, MN 55760

st. croix river

THE ST. CROIX, described as one of mid-America's most scenic rivers, actually is a part of two states—Wisconsin and Minnesota. It forms the boundary between the two for 120 of the 174 miles it courses from its source at Solon Springs, Wis., to its confluence with the Mississippi at Hastings, Minn.; the St. Croix is one of America's favorite and most natural canoe streams.

Despite occasional outbursts as it rushes over resistant remains of lava flows, the river's atmosphere is peaceful and serene. It's a stream of high banks, many sandy islands and sandbars and flows through a pristine area befitting any wilderness one can find in America. One of the finer safer stretches of fast water begins at Head-of-the-Rapids Island and stretches downstream past the Kettle River. At the Kettle River Rapids, the St. Croix divides into two parts, being joined by the Kettle River at the lower end. Below the rapids, the river widens from 300 to 1,200 feet with an average drop of slightly over one foot per mile and a maximum depth of from two to ten feet.

A glimpse of the St. Croix River, Minnesota—Wisconsin border

The stream is not totally without reminders of man, as you'll see when you reach Taylors Falls where a dam blocks the river forcing canoeists to portage. But it is a stream capable of obliging one a wilderness experience. The St. Croix above Taylors Falls to the dam at Gordon, and the Namekagon, a tributary, below Lake Namekagon, were selected as one of the initial eight rivers in the nation to be included in the National Wild and Scenic Rivers System. It is now administered by the National Park Service.

To reach the River: From St. Paul take I-35 north to SR 48 east to Danbury. This is a good place to start your river adventure. Other points are St. Croix State Park, reached via County Road 22, off SR 48, just a short distance downstream; Foot of Rapids Landing, just below the Kettle River.

WHERE TO DRIVE

No roads lead alongside the St. Croix, but there are some that periodically cross it including SR 48 near Danbury, US 8 near St. Croix Falls, and even I-94 just east of St. Paul. You'll find some other secondary roads, too, if you scout and explore the area, which makes for half the fun. Consult the National Park Service

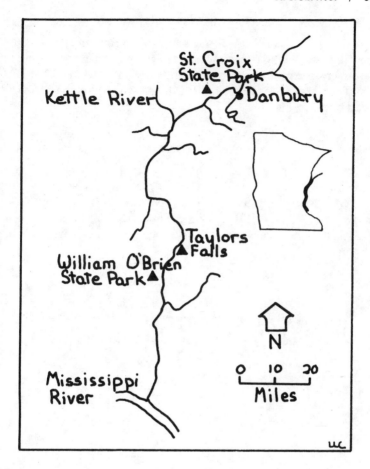

for their recommendations on points where you can best view the river.

WHERE TO HIKE

No hiking trails lead along the entirety of the river, but there are some trails which allow you to view spectacular stretches of it, particularly in the area of St. Croix State Park, Interstate State Park, and at William O'Brien State Park. Again consult the National Park Service for details on hiking the area.

BACKPACKING OPPORTUNITIES

Some of the trails lead close enough to the river to allow one to have a backpacking experience and to camp overnight. Be careful not to cross private property without first gaining permission to do so. In general—because of limited trails—this is not considered a good backpacking area.

WHERE TO CAMP

Camping is permitted on the islands and sandbars along the river as well as at several established campsites along the route. For established campsites, the St. Croix State Park, Interstate State Park, and William O'Brien State Park offer the best camping possibilities, although there are also some private campgrounds in the area.

Where to Obtain Information

Superintendent
St. Croix Nat'l Scenic River
P.O. Box 579
St. Croix Falls, WI 54024

upper mississippi river

wilderness

ALONG THE UPPER reaches of America's greatest river lies an area extending into Minnesota, Wisconsin, Iowa, and Illinois where the meandering stream is studded with wooded islands. It's in this area one finds the solitude and serenity that accompanies a wilderness experience and some 45,000 acres of territory fall in that category. Most of the area—195,000 acres—already is included in the Upper Mississippi River Fish and Wildlife Refuge. Although river navigation is open through this territory, the lowland and island areas of the upper Mississippi are largely unoccupied or influenced by man. Periodic flooding has kept it so.

Wildlife is abundant and the area is heavily vegetated with willow, silver maple, American elm, cottonwood, river birch, poplar, and several species of oaks, marsh flora, and bulrushes. Even though a lock and dam system harnesses the waterway, the visitor viewing the great valley from the bluffs or experiencing it by boat may find incomparable beauty much as early explorers saw it. The

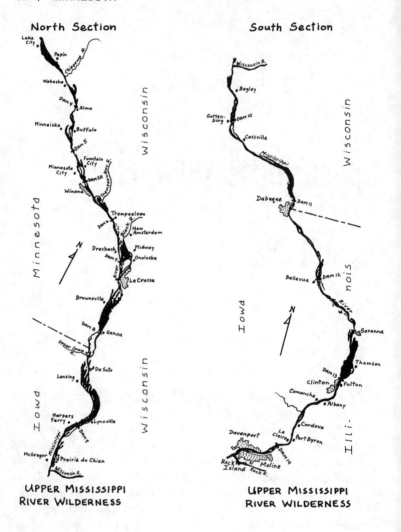

North Section

South Section

UPPER MISSISSIPPI
RIVER WILDERNESS

UPPER MISSISSIPPI
RIVER WILDERNESS

great cliffs still loom above the river and the carpet of woodlands is just as dense as ever.

The area is diverse, extending hundreds of miles along the river; it even contains differing life zones and climatic conditions. Some 270 bird species, 50 mammal and 113 fish species are found here.

Being along the Mississippi migratory waterfowl flyway, it attracts thousands upon thousands of Canada and snow geese, mallards, and other types of ducks in the spring and fall. They feed in the protected sloughs and shallows and nest among the trees. Wood ducks make their home and nesting grounds here. Also found are large rookeries of great blue herons, common egrets, bitterns, and rails. At few other places in North America will one find greater numbers of bald eagles wintering than here. Peregrine falcon and osprey are also found here. Other wildlife includes white-tailed deer, otter, beaver, mink, raccoon, skunk, fox and weasel, fox squirrels, jackrabbits and cottontail rabbits. A few nutria are found.

Fishing for walleye, sauger, largemouth bass, perch, sunfish species, and catfish is popular. One of the best areas for a wilderness experience is the Upper Reno Bottoms, near the Iowa-Minnesota line, a maze of old channels and wooded islands. Another such area is the Sny Magill area downstream from the entrance to the Wisconsin River. These are excellent canoe waters, but beware of canoeing in the main channel of the Mississippi, particularly on summer weekends. Pleasure boaters and water skiers are out in legion force. Also, one must be aware that tow boats and barges can be dangerous for canoeists and small boats, not only from over-running, but from the heavy wakes attending their passing.

To reach the area: You can get to this area from either side of the river. It extends from Lake City, Minnesota, to Rock Island, Illinois. Headquarters for the wildlife refuge is at Winona, Minnesota, and this should be your initial destination before attempting to experience the wilderness aspects of the area. At the headquarters you may obtain advice.

WHERE TO DRIVE

Best places to view this area—and they are mighty scenic ones, too—are on SR 35 between Prairie du Chien, and La Crosse, Wisconsin, and on US 61 from La Crescent to Red Wing, Minnesota. Also an excellent drive extends from Bluff Siding to the junction of US 63 on the Wisconsin side of the river. On all these roads are breathtaking vistas—nothing comparable to western scenery, of course—but scenery worth pulling off the road to enjoy. A section of SR 182 north of Lansing, Iowa, is also well worth your driving pleasure. Several roads lead across the Mississippi at various points along this route; choose your own for a rewarding route.

WHERE TO HIKE

Except for short nature trails for hiking in some of the state parks along the route, no lengthy trails exist in the area. One can, however, hike or backpack the backroads leading along the river (SR 35 in Wisconsin is excellent for that purpose since traffic is normally light except for weekends). This area is best experienced by canoe.

WHERE TO CANOE

Best places to canoe include Harper's Slough below Harper's Ferry, Iowa; Black River Bottoms near New Amsterdam, Wisconsin; Upper Reno Bottoms near the Iowa-Minnesota line, and Root River Bottoms near La Crosse, Wisconsin. Many other places are suitable for canoeing also, but after you've decided which area you wish to visit, contact refuge personnel for their recommendations on where you can best canoe. They can also recommend good launch and takeout points. You won't find whitewater here—the canoe experience is coupled with near dead paddling for the current is slow, particularly in the backwater areas.

BACKPACKING OPPORTUNITIES

Backpacking can be done wherever you undertake a hiking experience, planning your camp at almost any spot along the riverbank or at established campgrounds in state parks or in private parks along the route.

WHERE TO CAMP

Campgrounds located nearby are far too numerous to mention here. Many are available, both private, state, and municipal, along the Mississippi. Consult a campground guidebook for exact locations.

Where to Obtain Information

Refuge Manager
Upper Mississippi River Fish and Wildlife Refuge
P.O. Box 226
Winona, MN 55987

Regional Director
Bureau of Sportfisheries and Wildlife
Federal Bldg., Fort Snelling
Twin Cities, MN 55111

voyageurs national park

WHILE VOYAGEURS NATIONAL Park, one of the newest in the nation, is not necessarily a wilderness, it can provide a wilderness-type experience. Made up mostly of huge lakes dotted with islands, it's similar in many ways to the International Boundary Waters Canoe Area. But here boats are allowed in addition to canoes. Although still in the development stage, this park will eventually encompass 219,400 acres. There are bogs, sand beaches, and cliffs.

The interior of Kabetogama peninsula has numbers of lakes reachable only on foot. Not only does this park offer a wilderness experience, but one associated with history and the colorful French *voyageur* who once inhabited this land. The country looks much the same today as it did during the days of the *voyageur* and one needs but to enter this place to sense the vastness and endless system of internal waterways framed in places by giant pine, spruce, fir, aspen, and birch.

To reach the Park: The Park is located quite close to Interna-

(NPS Photo by Larry Knowles)

Shoreline scene at western end of Lake Kabetogama, Minnesota

tional Falls, to the east and southeast. From Duluth, Minn., take US 53 north to St. Louis County Road 23 from Orr, Ash River Trail, St. Louis County Road or to Minn. Highway 11 east.

WHERE TO DRIVE

While to see this park, you must take to the water, several roads do lead along the southern boundary with dead-end roads leading to the park at Sullivan Bay, Kabetogama Lake and State Point. Other roads likely will be constructed into some areas as more of the park is developed, so it's a good idea to check with the park superintendent prior to your visit. County Road 122 just south of International Falls provides access to the south shore of Lake Kabetogama; SH 11 from International Falls to park at Black Bay and Neil Point; Ash River Trail to Namakan Lake.

WHERE TO HIKE

A few hiking trails have been established in the area, but there are other areas into which you can hike from a boat camp, particu-

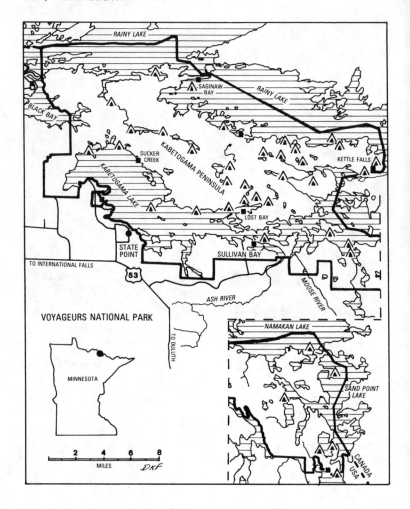

larly on the Kabetogama Peninsula. This will give you an opportunity to explore at will as did the *voyageurs*, and sense some identity with them and their experiences.

BACKPACKING OPPORTUNITIES

Backpacking experience is primitive at several inland lakes on the Kabetogama Peninsula. Find your own way to established campsites on inland lakes. Water may be used from most of them for drinking and cooking. Fishing is excellent for northern pike, walleye, trout, and bass.

WHERE TO CAMP

Many boat campsites (all primitive) have been established throughout the area. Most of them are on Namakan Lake and the Kabetogama Peninsula. Others are on smaller lakes on the peninsula. Consult the park map issued at the headquarters for specific locations. Camping facilities near the park area are provided by the U.S. Forest Service and the State of Minnesota.

Where to Get Information

Park Superintendent
P.O. Box 50
International Falls, MN 56649

NORTH DAKOTA

chase lake wilderness

LYING IN THAT part of North Dakota known as the Coteau section of the Missouri Plateau is Chase Lake National Wildlife Refuge which contains a 4,155-acre wilderness. Most of the wilderness is characteristic of the general area with many closed depressions which are part of the pitted outwash plain of a receded glacier. Called potholes, they contain water to sustain numerous species of wildlife to include white pelicans, which is the main purpose for this refuge's existence. Other forms of wildlife include the slate-colored junco and sharp-tailed grouse, double-crested cormorant, ring-billed gull, California gull, the white-tailed jackrabbit, white-tailed deer, sandhill cranes, Canada geese, whistling swans, badger, mink, coyote, Hungarian partridge, skunk, and ground squirrels. Many ducks nest and rear their young annually on this refuge. The white pelican colony, located within the wilderness area, is perhaps the largest in the world. Because of the dense population, they range out many miles searching for

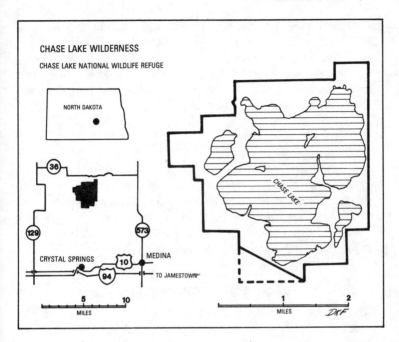

food, and will be seen in graceful flight trading in and out of the area.

The land here is generally level to sloping; it is semi-arid, with less than 18 inches of rainfall annually. Winds blow continually and temperatures may range from such extremes as 120 degrees in the summer to 42 below zero during winter.

The refuge was established by President Teddy Roosevelt in 1908 and is managed by the Arrowwood National Wildlife Refuge at Edmunds, some 27 miles east and 16 miles north of Chase Lake.

To reach Chase Lake: From Medina take SR 573 north and turn west to the refuge.

WHERE TO DRIVE

Hwy. 30 leads north and south along the eastern portion of Chase Lake, Hwy. 36 east and west along the northern side. From these roads, particularly early in the morning and late in the afternoons, you can spot considerable wildlife plus seeing the white pelicans in flight. The latter alone make the trip worthwhile, particularly if you're a bird fancier, since they constitute the largest concentration of white pelicans anyplace on the globe. For other routes, consult refuge personnel at the Arrowhead National Wildlife Refuge, just down the road.

WHERE TO HIKE

No established trails exist in this wilderness, but since it is prairie country, you may easily find your own path around the lake or refuge area. Beware of rattlers and be sure to carry a snakebite and first-aid kit. You may also want to carry binoculars and a canteen of water. With these, you can exploit one of the finest bird watching opportunities in Mid-America.

BACKPACKING OPPORTUNITIES

Backpacking is permitted on the refuge, but overnight camping is not, mainly to avoid disturbing the wildlife, particularly the white pelicans.

WHERE TO CAMP

Camping spots are tough to come by in this part of North Dakota. When I was there, I had luck in getting permission to camp from an obliging rancher at a primitive site. The nearest other campground is located some 70 miles south at Beaver Lake just off SR 30. A KOA campground is located on US 2 near Devils Lake some 70 miles north of the refuge.

Where to Obtain Information

Refuge Manager
Arrowwood Nat'l Wildlife Refuge
Edmunds, ND 58434

theodore roosevelt
national park

THE THEODORE ROOSEVELT National Park of North Dakota, established in 1947, covers some 110 square miles of the most rugged country in the upper Midwest. Space here is so broad one feels he can almost reach the stars on a summer night. Much of the area is Badlands straddling some 200 miles of the Little Missouri River. Life is fragile here because of arid conditions and users of the park, particularly the back-country wilderness, are urged to use extreme caution with fires. Rainfall comes mostly during May through July, but averages only about 15 inches annually.

Enough moisture is retained in riverbanks and ravines to sustain small groves of cottonwood trees, which offer food and shelter for white-tailed and mule deer. Other wildlife includes rabbits, beaver, porcupines, raccoons, prairie dogs, coyotes, bobcats, golden eagles, and a number of reptiles including western diamondback rattlers. One small herd of wild horses roams the area and there are wild buffalo, antelope, and bighorn sheep, although the latter are rarely seen.

Buffalo grazing in the Theodore Roosevelt National Memorial Park, North Dakota

This country was one of former President Teddy Roosevelt's favorite spots, hence it was named after him. The park is open all year, but the best time to visit is from May through September. The climate here is rugged during the winter months and snows often come as early as October and continue through April and into early May. The park is split into two units—north and south—located some ten miles apart. Both offer a most unusual wilderness experience.

To reach the Park: From Belfield, take I-95 and US 10 west past Painted Canyon to Medora, location of the park headquarters.

WHERE TO DRIVE

While each of the two units are similar in terrain features and wildlife, they must be considered separately. First, in the south unit, stop at the museum to learn something of the natural history and background of the area. The restored Maltese Cross Cabin used by Teddy Roosevelt on his visits here has been relocated behind the museum and is open to the public.

Enroute to the park, stop at the Painted Canyon Overlook at Exit 8, some seven miles east of Medora. Here you have a magnificent view of the Badlands topography and colors. Restrooms, picnic shelters, tables, fireplaces, and water are available.

Once you've left the headquarters armed with literature, maps, and recommendations by park personnel, take the 38-mile Scenic Loop Road. A number of significant park features are marked along the way such as Scoria Point, (massive bluffs capped with red scoria show the place where a vein of lignite coal burned away and baked the surrounding sand and clay, converting it into brick); Badlands Overlook Buck Hill (highest point in the park at 2,855 feet); Wind Canyon and Peaceful Valley. Some of the road parallels the Little Missouri River and one may, provided water levels are sufficient, canoe this stream through the park or float it in rafts.

In the north unit, the Scenic Drive starts at the entrance station and ends at Sperati Point 13 miles later, with several turnouts and interpretative signs. (Caution: Do not take trailers beyond the Squaw Creek Campground.) Here you'll find a small herd of wild long-horn cattle, descendants of those driven north from Texas on the Long Trail crossing the park. Other features include Slump Block, Squaw Creek Nature Trail (½ mile loop); Caprock Coulee Nature Trail (1.5 miles) and Sperati Point, narrowest gateway in the Badlands.

Most of the drives in the park, not considering the points of interest, are bounded by vast wilderness. You need not use imagination to realize that change in this land is unnoticeable, even after the passage of a hundred years.

WHERE TO HIKE

An extensive system of back-country trails are found throughout both units of the park and hikers are also invited to strike out cross-country wherever they feel the urge to roam. Any park visitor is invited to leave his car at one of the roadside pull-outs and explore the Badlands on foot. Not all the trails are developed and marked, thus one should have topographic maps and a compass

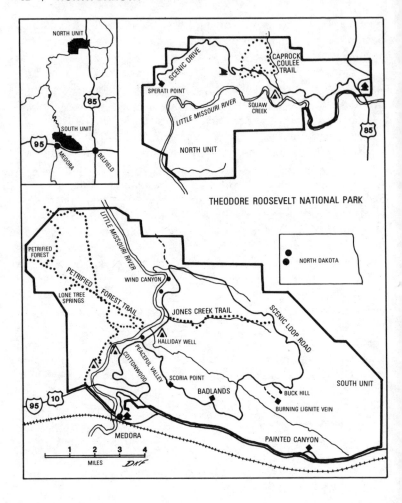

and be proficient in reading them before going very deep into the wilderness.

One of the most popular trails is the Petrified Forest Trail, extending some five miles northwest from the vicinity of the Peaceful Valley Ranch. Approximately half-way along the trail, a spur leads to Lone Tree Springs, but its water should be either boiled or chemically treated before use. Other trails include the Jones Creek

Trail (4 miles) in the South Unit and Caprock Coulee Trail in the North Unit (5 mile loop). Other unmarked trails are available for hikers, but first inquire for information on them at the park headquarters.

One may hike for weeks in the Badlands backcountry without seeing another person, provided you can carry enough provisions. Water points are plentiful.

BACKPACKING OPPORTUNITIES

Major detriments to backpacking are a hot arid climate in summer and a cold snowy one in winter. Temperatures may range up to 100 degrees in summer with little shade. Make sure to carry water and an ample supply of salt tablets. Backpacking is permitted in all parts of the park, either on established or non-established trails. Beware of rattlers, buffalo, and long-horn cattle. Stay a good distance from them. Wild horses and other wildlife pose no threat. Either boil or chemically treat your water. Be sure to register with Park Headquarters before packing in.

WHERE TO CAMP

Primitive camping is permitted throughout the park except within one-half mile of any park road. Established campgrounds are located at Cottonwood and Halliday Well in the South Unit and at Squaw Creek in the North Unit. Also there are private campgrounds within a 50-mile drive of the park. Again, campers are urged to be particularly careful of fires and not to molest the wildlife or collect any materials such as rocks, fossils, etc.

WHERE TO CANOE

Virtually all the Little Missouri River in the park area is suitable for canoeing and it makes a nice canoe float trip. The current is slow. Early in the morning and late in the evening are excellent times to view wildlife coming to the stream for water. Many spots for setting up a primitive camp, some in groves of cottonwood trees, are available.

Where to Obtain Information

Superintendent
Theodore Roosevelt Nat'l Park
Medora, ND 58645

OHIO

archers fork wilderness

SITUATED IN THE midst of the Wayne National Forest, this 19,000-acre proposed wilderness area offers an excellent opportunity to be alone. Only about 7,000 acres of the area is open to the public at this writing; the remainder being privately owned. Embracing an area of high hills with steep inclines and sharp hollows interspersed with small streams, the area possesses great beauty and charm.

In the center of the area is Archers Fork Creek and along the western boundary is one of the most pristine streams in Ohio—the Little Muskingum River, an excellent canoe stream. Fishing for smallmouth bass and bream is good to excellent. Good launch and takeout points are available all along the Little Muskingum. Wildlife includes wild turkey, white-tailed deer, fox, raccoon, and many smaller species.

To reach the area: Take SR 26 northeast out of Marietta to the small village of Dart, located on the edge of the wilderness. To

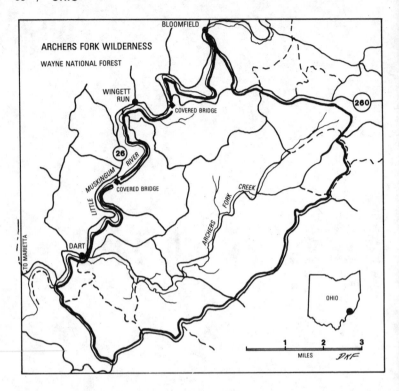

float the Little Muskingum past the wilderness, drive on to Bloomfield and launch.

WHERE TO DRIVE

Several roads presently lead into the area east out of Dart, but they likely will be closed off once the area is established a wilderness. Also one may drive the perimeter route by taking SR 26 and SR 260 along the west and north sides.

WHERE TO HIKE

No hiking trails have been established, but the area is open to hikers and no difficulty need be anticipated in blazing your own trail. Several dirt roads are located in the area and are excellent for hiking.

BACKPACKING OPPORTUNITIES

Backpacking is permissable on public lands in the area as long as one properly respects the natural environment.

WHERE TO CAMP

No established campsites are located in the wilderness area, but one may camp along Archers Fork Creek at a place of his own choosing. Other campsites may be found along the Little Muskingum River. Established campgrounds are located in the nearby national forestlands. Check with Ranger Headquarters, U.S. Forest Service, Marietta, Ohio, for maps and directions to those.

Where to Obtain Information

Ranger Headquarters
U.S. Forest Service
Marietta, OH 45750

Supervisor
Hoosier-Wayne Nat'l Forest
U.S. Forest Service
1615 J St.
Bedford, IN 47421

shawnee wilderness area

IN HIGH HILL country of southeast Ohio is the 5,000-acre
Shawnee Wilderness, heavily forested with red oak, white oak,
walnut, gum maple, hickory, and dogwood. The area is bisected by
numerous small streams in deep ravines and hollows. Wildlife here
includes wild turkey, grouse, white-tailed deer, timber rattlesnakes
and copperheads, pileated woodpeckers, and numerous owls and
hawks. Sometimes called Ohio's Little Smokies, the area borders
the Shawnee State Forest and State Park which offers a multitude
of activities including camping, hunting, nature trails, bridle trails,
and fishing.

To reach the area: From east or west, take US 52 to Friendship.
The Forest Headquarters is located directly east of Friendship on
US 52 while a Ranger Station adjacent to the wilderness is located
directly east of Buena Vista, also on US 52.

WHERE TO DRIVE

Motorists can completely circle the wilderness area and have the option of making frequent stops and walk-ins for short distances enroute. About half the area is bounded by FR 17 on the west; US 52 is on the south and FR 2 and Upper Twin Creek Road bounds the eastern portion. At Twin Creek Fire Tower, one may find the opportunity to climb for a look at the entire area.

WHERE TO HIKE

Abandoned roads are available for hiking through the wilderness area. The understory of the woodland is generally open, particularly in fall, winter, and early spring, and hikers are welcome to enter the woodland. Beware of poisonous snakes during warm weather. The adjacent Shawnee State Forest offers 20 miles of hiking and backpacking trails through the woodland. Most popular is Panorama Trail which follows a high ridge through the most spectacular portion of the forest.

BACKPACKING OPPORTUNITIES

Backpackers are allowed to hike and camp by permit on the backpack trail and in designated campsites but are strongly urged to leave the forest unmarked and undisturbed by their visit. No established campsites are available and there's no drinking water. During dry seasons, there's virtually no water at all. Drinking water is provided along the backpack trail at several points in the Forest, but none in the wilderness itself.

WHERE TO CAMP

Campgrounds, lodge accommodations and cabins are located in nearby forest and park areas.

Where to Obtain Information

Forest Headquarters
Box 8
Friendship, OH 45630

Division of Forests and Preserves
Dept. of Natural Resources
Fountain Square
Columbus, OH 43224

stark wilderness center

THIS MINI-WILDERNESS, containing only about 500 acres, provides a refreshing experience. Organized by the Canton, Ohio Audubon Society in 1963, the center is actually a living museum including 30 acres of virgin timber on the edge of a glaciated area. Here are found giant beech, maple, oak, and hickory trees.

The Boy Scouts and other volunteer groups help to maintain the mini-wilderness and it has become a popular outdoor classroom for students. A sign at the entrance leading to a complex of trails says it best: "Protected by man but managed by nature, visitors are welcome to learn, to enjoy, but not to disturb. Do not enter with gun, dog, ax, knife, trap or wire."

Wildlife includes skunk, the rare flying squirrel, quail, pheasant, raccoon, groundhog, cottontail rabbits, and other small inhabitants.

To reach the area: Take US 62 west of Wilmot and Canton and follow sign to Stark Wilderness.

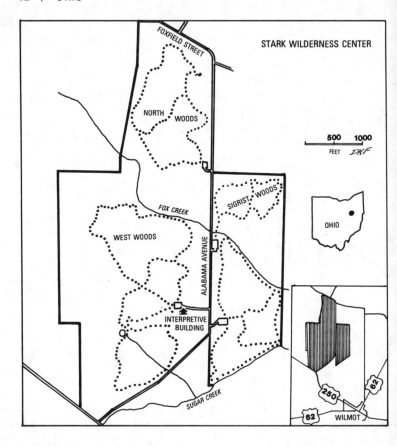

WHERE TO DRIVE

Only the road leading to the Interpretative Building at the area headquarters is open to automotive traffic.

WHERE TO HIKE

Near the edge of the glaciated area is a winding loop trail three-fourths mile long with a shorter trail one-third mile inside it. Along the Sigrist Trail are giant trees, among them a burr oak 16 feet in diameter, a butternut hickory, runner-up to the state champion, 114 feet high; and a red maple which holds the Ohio state record.

The North Woods Trail heads past Warbler Point, a spot popular during spring and fall bird migrations. All trails are short but interesting.

BACKPACKING OPPORTUNITIES

No backpacking is allowed here.

WHERE TO CAMP

No camping is allowed at the wilderness center, but there are some private campgrounds within a hour's drive of the center. Check your campground directory or consult the Ohio Travel Division.

Where to Obtain Information

Travel Division
Dept. of Economic Development
State Office Bldg.
Columbus, OH 43215

Superintendent
Stark Wilderness Center
Wilmot, OH 44689

west sister island
national wildlife refuge

FOR YEARS THIS has been a place of refuge for boaters dating back to Indian times during storms on Lake Erie. The mid-lake location of this 85-acre island gives it a climate exceptionally free from great daily temperature fluctuations. It appears flat-topped but actually rises 35 feet above the lake. Virtually all the island is forested, the trees interspersed with a few tiny ponds in the interior. A few acres are open grasslands fringed with chokeberry and wild plum.

A lighthouse operated by the U. S. Coast Guard stands on the westward-most portion of the island, but otherwise man's intrusion is not evident. Near the lighthouse is a broad landing beach where boats may put to shore.

Wildlife includes blue herons, black crowned night herons, and common egrets. These birds have more than 1,100 active nests perched in the tops of hackberry trees on the north half of the island. Not enough food is found on the island to sustain them,

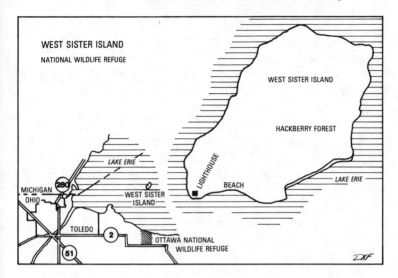

however, necessitating several round trips daily to the mainland 18 miles away to gather food. The bald eagle has been known to nest here. Smaller birds include swallows, purple martins, song sparrows, warblers and red-winged blackbirds.

The rock ledges bordering the lake make ideal habitat for numerous snakes including water snakes, blacksnakes, and blue racers. The herons and egrets require solitude during the nesting season, thus visitors to the island are discouraged during the spring and early summer period.

How to reach the Island: Drive to Oak Harbor, Ohio via SR 163 east of Toledo where you should check at the National Wildlife Refuge headquarters for information. West Sister can be reached only by boat nine miles off the south shore. Beware of treacherous Lake Erie where wind can change the temperament of the lake within minutes.

WHERE TO DRIVE

No roads are on the island and no means are available for getting your automobile to it. Best way to see the island is to boat around it; excellent for bird watching from boat.

WHERE TO HIKE

No camping facilities are located on the island, but there are several on the mainland in the vicinity of Oak Harbor including a couple of state parks. Camping is also available on nearby South Bass Island and also on Kelley's Island.

Where to Obtain Information

Refuge Manager
West Sister Island Nat'l Wildlife Refuge
Oak Harbor, OH 43449

INDIANA

nebo ridge wilderness

IN THE NORTHERN edge of the Hoosier National Forest of southern Indiana's hill country is Nebo Ridge, an area in excess of 15,000 acres of wooded wilderness with high steep ridges and sharp ravines. Lake Monroe, largest man-made lake in Indiana, partially bounds the wilderness area; another edge adjoins the southern boundary of Brown County State Park, the largest such park in Indiana. It is a complex region of jumbled ridges and valleys.

Two of the large creek systems, which comprise the watershed for Lake Monroe, flow through the area. Small streams are numerous, many with sandstone bottoms and steep ridges rising sharply on either side. Geodes are common in many of the streams and the surrounding countryside. Fern-covered slopes graced with native hardwoods—hickory, yellow poplar, white oak, red oak, sycamore, and many supporting wild grapevines as huge as a man's wrist—mark the transition between stream valley and ridgetop.

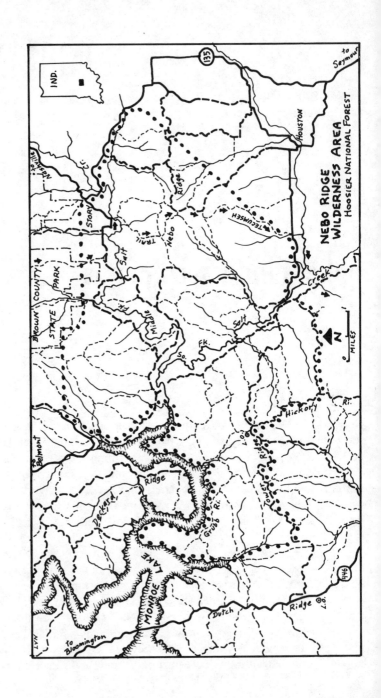

Wildlife here includes ruffed grouse, wild turkey, osprey, bald eagle, bobcat, raccoon, opossum, cottontail rabbit, white-tailed deer, and fox. Roadless areas also are found adjacent to the wilderness in Brown County State Park and in Yellowwood State Forest, together comprising some 40,000 acres of wild lands. Beware: The habitat includes timber rattlers and copperheads.

To reach the Wilderness: Take SR 135 south from Nashville to the small hamlet of Story, on the eastern edge of the wilderness.

WHERE TO DRIVE

Numerous roads bound the wilderness area. Along the tailwaters of Lake Monroe is Elkinsville Road which leads past Browning Mountain, the highest point in the wilderness. Mt. Nebo Road and the Houston Road also are good ones to follow. For a detailed map of those roads in Brown County, consult the Brown County Chamber of Commerce, Nashville. For other areas in other adjoining counties, consult the District Ranger, Brownstown Ranger Station, Brownstown, Ind. For detailed hiking maps, secure USGS topographic quadrangle maps.

WHERE TO HIKE

Although one may virtually choose his own way in these woodlands, following largely the ridges (particularly in late fall and winter), one main trail leads through the area. Called the Tecumseh Trail, it runs north and south and is part of an extensive system running from the Ohio River northward to the Morgan Monroe State Forest. For details on this and other trails, contact the North American Trail Complex, P.O. Box 805, Bloomington, IN 47401.

BACKPACKING OPPORTUNITIES

Backpackers will find this ideal country for a challenging experience. Follow the ridges and the going is fairly easy. But to get to the streams, one must climb down steep embankments. Although the water is usable, it's best to either boil or chemically treat it. Choose your own campsite; there are no established ones.

WHERE TO CAMP

Nearest organized camping is either at the Hardin Ridge Recreation Area on Lake Monroe in the National Forest, the Brown County State Park or at a KOA campground on SR 46 near Gnawbone, a few miles north of the wilderness. In the wilderness area, choose your own campsite wherever you find suitable conditions.

Where to Obtain Information

Forest Supervisor
Hoosier Nat'l Forest
Bedford, IN 47421

District Ranger
U.S. Forest Service
Brownstown, IN 47220

ILLINOIS

crab orchard wilderness

JUST FIFTY MILES north of the confluence of the Mississippi and Ohio Rivers, Crab Orchard Wilderness is part of the Crab Orchard National Wildlife Refuge. Comprising 4,050 acres of the 43,970-acre refuge, the area lies around the southern perimeters of Little Grassy and Devil's Kitchen lakes in the southern portion of the refuge. Both of these lakes provide some of the best largemouth bass and crappie fishing in all of Illinois (some nine-pounder largemouth have been taken from each of these lakes).

Homesteading, farming, and logging have occurred on portions of the area in the past, but during the last 20 years or so, nature has largely restored these areas to wilderness status. The south boundary of the area joins the Shawnee National Forest. Three long arms of Devil's Kitchen Lake and two of Little Grassy protrude into the area with shorelines preserved in a most natural state.

Canoes can be used to explore this portion of the wilderness. Wildlife here includes snapping turtles, king snakes, copperhead,

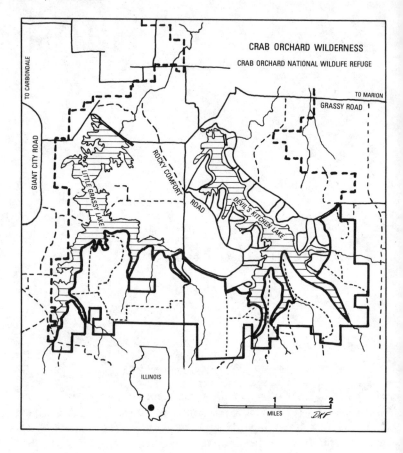

wild turkey, white-tailed deer, and bobcat. During late fall and winter, thousands of Canada and snow geese and a multitude of wild ducks congregate at the Crab Orchard Refuge, often to spend the winter. This is on the Mississippi Flyway for waterfowl. With the geese and ducks also come golden and bald eagles.

To reach the refuge: From Marion, take SR 13 west to SR 148 south which leads past Refuge Headquarters. Here you should seek literature and directions to the wilderness area.

WHERE TO DRIVE

Several roads bound the wilderness area including Giant City Road leading south out of Carbondale, Grassy Road along the northern border, and Rockey Comfort Road between Little Grassy Lake and Devil's Kitchen Lake. All these roads provide excellent opportunities for viewing wildlife as well as acquainting the motorist with the wilderness aspects of this southern Illinois country.

WHERE TO HIKE

The woodlands in this area are not dense enough to preclude hiking almost anywhere one wishes to go. In addition, there are several old abandoned roads in the area which provide excellent hiking opportunities. Consult the refuge headquarters for details and exact locations.

BACKPACKING OPPORTUNITIES

Backpackers are welcome in the wilderness area. Water from either of the lakes may be used if boiled or chemically treated and campsites, although primitive, are ideal along some of the abandoned roads.

WHERE TO CAMP

Choose your own campsite in the primitive area, although it's a good idea to pick one more than a quarter of a mile from public roadways. Also private-concession campgrounds are operated on both Devil's Kitchen and Little Grassy lakes. Water is available at each plus rental boats for fishing, bait, accessories, etc.

Where to Obtain Information

Refuge Manager
Crab Orchard Nat'l Wildlife Refuge
P.O. Box J
Carterville, IL 62918

la rue-pine hills ecological area

HERE ARE UNIQUE examples of interrelationships that exist between species of plants and animals with great diversity of life forms, some rare and endangered species. More than 40 rare species of plants are found within the area. The Pine Hills overlook the Mississippi River valley and provide a number of striking scenic views. Comprising 1,996 acres in the Shawnee National Forest, it's characterized by flat river bottom, backwater swamp and the limestone bluffs of the Pine Hills which rise some 350 feet abruptly above the LaRue Swamp.

The Pine Hills area is a veritable natural rock garden with a gross display of wild flowers throughout the spring and summer. Wildlife includes beaver, white-tailed deer, bobcat, bald eagle, the eastern woodrat, and many species of reptiles including cotton-mouth snakes, rattlers, and copperhead. Two rare sunfish—the dwarf and the pigmy sunfish—and the spring cavefish are present in streams leading to the swamp. The Indiana bat—an endangered

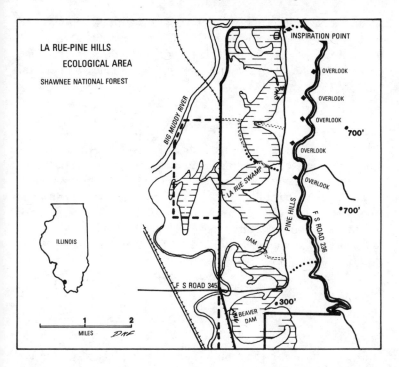

species—still inhabits the bluffs and occasionally a peregrine falcon, considered almost extinct east of the Mississippi, visits the area.

The entire ecological area, while affording a most unique wilderness experience, is small and never far away from the inroads of civilization. It's also fragile and will not condone abuse in any way from the public, so all who visit here are urged to take special care not to damage plants nor disturb animal life. Even footprints off the trails or road areas are too much to leave.

To reach the area: Take SR 3 south out of East St. Louis past Grand Tower to Forest Service Road 345, which leads directly through the area.

WHERE TO DRIVE

Approximately three miles of FS Road 345 (gravel) leads immediately between the swamp and the pine bluffs allowing the motorist to sample both at the same time. There are pulloff areas and short trails where motorists can take mini-hikes. Branching off from 345 is FS Road 236 which leads to the crest of the Pine Bluffs and winds along them approximately six miles with several pulloff areas and excellent vistas.

WHERE TO HIKE

Hiking is limited, but Inspiration Point Trail (three-fourths mile) provides the hiker an opportunity to interpret some of the interesting features of the Pine Hills, leading along a dry narrow ridge and downward into a deep, cool valley. The vista at Inspiration Point is one of the most scenic in Illinois. Near the western end of the swamp is a dirt road which connects with a stretch of railroad good for hiking, a distance of one and a quarter miles. Both FS roads mentioned normally have only light traffic and are good for hiking, particularly on weekdays.

BACKPACKING OPPORTUNITIES

Because of the fragile nature of the area, backpacking is permitted but no overnight camping unless backpackers wish to use established Pine Hills campground just south of the area on FS Road 236.

WHERE TO CAMP

Pine Hills campground, operated by the U.S. Forest Service, offers 12 sites with drinking water and pit toilets. Summer weekends are usually crowded.

Where to Obtain Information

Supervisor
Shawnee Nat'l Forest
U.S. Forest Service
Harrisburg, IL 62946

MISSOURI

black mingo nature area

THIS ECOLOGICAL WILDERNESS, just 1,700 acres in size, is part of the Mingo National Wildlife Refuge in southeastern Missouri. It lies in an abandoned channel of the Mississippi River between the foothills of the Ozarks on the west and the uplands of Crowley's Ridge on the east.

At one time attempts were made to drain this swamp and farm it, but after many millions of dollars spent and the failure of the effort, it reverted back to a veritable wilderness. Not without scar from those efforts, the swamp nonetheless has recovered quickly and wildlife is everywhere. Refuge access is restricted, however, during the October 1 to March 15 period to minimize disturbance to migrating waterfowl which use the area and sometimes winter here.

White-tailed deer can be seen at any time of year. Other wildlife includes bobcat, gray fox, swamp rabbit, raccoon, shortail shrew, beaver, coyote, wild turkey, mink, and possibly river otter. More than a dozen species of ducks, Canada and snow geese, and oc-

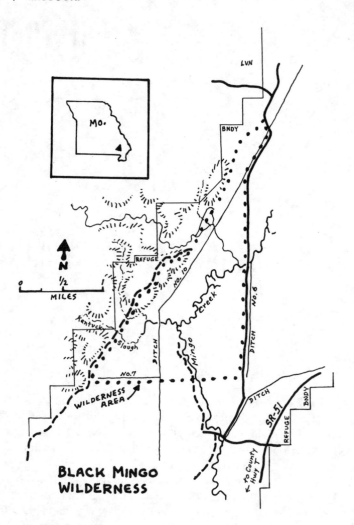

BLACK MINGO
WILDERNESS

casionally the bald eagle are seen here. While the entire wildlife refuge, which contains some 22,000 acres, is most interesting, it is only the Black Mingo Nature Area (some 1,700 acres) this writer feels begins to qualify for a wilderness experience. Warning: Cottonmouth moccasins, rattlesnakes, and copperhead snakes also make this their home.

Fishing is excellent for buffalo, crappie, and largemouth bass on the refuge and in the nature area. Trees here include bald cypress, pin oak, and willow oak in addition to a number of others.

To reach the Refuge: From Puxico, take SR 51 northeast 1.5 miles to the refuge headquarters. Puxico is located 45 miles southwest of Cape Girardeau in southeastern Missouri.

WHERE TO DRIVE

County Road T leads along the southern border of the refuge; SR 51 along the eastern side. County Road Z leads to the northern end of the nature area and a point from which you can hike into the area. A refuge road also leads off County Road T to the Black Mingo River along the southern perimeter of the nature area—a good place to launch a canoe.

During the months of October and November, the refuge is open to self-guided auto tours each Sunday afternoon. This marked tour route is about 25 miles long and takes some two to three hours to complete. Any organized group of ten or more people may arrange for a conducted lecture tour any day of the week by contacting the refuge office.

WHERE TO HIKE

Hiking is permitted throughout the refuge providing one a great opportunity to view wildlife and enjoy the serenity of a natural setting. Although there's water along the way, don't drink it. Bring your own. The hike provides an excellent day-long experience. Be sure to take a good insect repellent along for mosquitoes and gnats are bothersome.

BACKPACKING OPPORTUNITIES

Since the refuge allows no overnight camping, backpacking is not permitted.

WHERE TO CANOE

A canoe route extending between two and three miles along Stanley Creek and Black Mingo River through the nature area provides an excellent opportunity to view wildlife and experience what wilderness was once like in this part of Missouri along the Mississippi River. Some backtracking may be necessary, but this is a good slow-water canoe trail and one of the best methods for entering the nature area.

WHERE TO CAMP

Although no camping nor overnight use is permitted on the refuge, there is camping on adjacent Wappapello Reservoir and in the Duck Creek Wildlife Management Area. One of the best places is the Sam A. Baker State Park on the northern end of Wappapello Reservoir. Other campgrounds are located nearby also; check with the refuge headquarters for their recommendations.

Where to Obtain Information

Refuge Manager
Mingo Nat'l Wildlife Refuge
Rte. 1, Box 9A
Puxico, MO 63960

current wild river

WANDERING DOWN THROUGH the Ozarks of southeastern Missouri are the nation's first designated national wild and scenic rivers—the Current and Jacks Fork. After 15 years of study, the National Park Service established 100 miles along the Current and 40 miles along one of its major tributaries—the Jacks Fork—as the Ozark National Scenic Riverways. Early French trappers named the river La Riviere Courante or "the running river," but this was later anglicized into "The Current River."

The river sweeps through a variety of terrain ranging from rugged to placid in the Ozark hills. Wildlife is plentiful. More than 200 species of birds including the pileated woodpecker, green heron, kingfisher, great blue heron, wood thrush, wild turkey, and six kinds of owl occupy the area. There are also white-tailed deer, opposum, raccoon, bobcat, rabbit, squirrel, red and gray fox, muskrat, mink, and beaver. Also present, but seldom seen, are wolves, badger, and black bear.

More than 1,500 plant species have been identified here. Few places in America are as rich in types of hardwood trees, grasses, shrubs, and wild flowers. Along the slopes of the river, you'll find oak, pine, hickory, gum, dogwood and redbud, sycamore, cottonwood, maple, and birch. More than 90 species of fish live in the Current and Jacks Fork rivers; most common are smallmouth and rock bass, yellow suckers, drum, red horse, channel cat and carp, walleye pike, and pickerel. Some of the walleye (they're known locally as Jack salmon) go as high as 20 pounds.

Springs are located all along the river and you can drink from them. In fact, it's claimed this stream has more freshwater springs than any other river in the nation, with the one possible exception of the Snake in Idaho and Wyoming. The Current is born at Montauk Spring and until it meets the White River in Arkansas, it is mostly spring-fed. Most impressive is Big Springs, largest single-orifice spring on the continent, which flows about 25-million gallons per day. Caves are all along the stream. The largest is Round Spring Cavern. Many of the caves along the river are unexplored and uncharted. Many sinks and potholes also are located along the way. Some are like chimney shafts up to 300 feet deep. Others are funnel-shaped holes several hundred feet in diameter and up to 70 feet deep.

The area is not crowded from mid-April through October. Winters are mild, however, and a good time to take a float on the stream. Annual rainfall is around 40 inches. Several canoe rentals are located along both rivers. It's an ideal canoe stream and is generally not considered dangerous.

To reach the Current: From Rolla, take US 63 south to SR 137, then turn shortly onto the Montauk Road. The Current is considered to begin here.

WHERE TO DRIVE

No roads follow or parallel the Current or the Jacks Fork. But SR 19, US 160 cross over it as it wends its way toward Arkansas. At these points, you can stop your car and drink in the atmosphere of this wild river. You may also find a few secondary or gravel roads that lead near or across the river at other points, too. Consult the Park Service for recommendations on the best places to drive to see it. At Powder Mill where SR 106 crosses the Current, is the Park Service Visitor Center.

WHERE TO HIKE

This is a float stream and only limited opportunities exist for you to hike along any portion of it. Check with the Park Service for locations of any foot paths which may allow you to sample parts of the river from the bank.

BACKPACKING OPPORTUNITIES

Backpacking here can best be combined with canoeing or john-boating down the river. Primitive campsites are numerous along the river; choose your spot. But during the crowded summer months, you may find some difficulty because of the river's popularity. Go to high ground during rain-flooding.

WHERE TO CAMP

An established campground is located at Montauk State Park near the beginning of the Current. Many primitive sites exist all along the Current and Jacks Fork. For specific places, consult the Park Service personnel upon arrival. Other campgrounds are nearby in the Mark Twain National Forest portion of the stream.

Where to Obtain Information

Park Superintendent
Ozark Nat'l Scenic Riverways
Van Buren, MO 63965

Missouri Tourism Comm.
308 E. High St.
Jefferson City, MO 65101

eleven point scenic river

IN SOUTHEASTERN MISSOURI not far from the Current and Jacks Fork Scenic Waterways is the Eleven Point Scenic River, administered by the U.S. Forest Service. The 45-mile section designated flows through a portion of the Mark Twain National Forest, extending from Thomasville to SR 142. Because it is one of the most scenic streams in the nation, because it is representative of a highland Ozark river and because it is a great waterway for canoeing and floating, the Eleven Point is indeed in many ways well worth preserving as a natural unmolested stream.

A focal point of activity on the river is Greer Crossing where SR 19 crosses the stream. A ford once used by Indians and horse-drawn wagons, it is now the starting point for many float trips. Old Greer Mill, still standing on the hilltop south of the crossing, was powered by a unique cable system running from a waterwheel in the spring branch. Greer Spring, flowing over one mile through a forest-clad gorge, is the second largest spring in Missouri. While there are—as

Running a short stretch of white water on the Eleven Point River, Missouri

at Greer's Mill—indications of man's influence upon the land, it still is by and large a wild river and worthy of a wilderness experience.

Wildlife along the way include kingfishers, pileated woodpeckers, and great blue herons. You also may see white-tailed deer, beaver, muskrat, mink and an occasional coyote. Bobcat and black bear also occupy the area. Cottonmouth, rattlesnakes, and copperhead also are found here, so beware. At night the area comes alive with the sounds of the wilderness, an experience never to be forgotten.

Fishing is excellent here, too, for smallmouth bass, sunfish, and rainbow trout. A series of vast underground reservoirs supply more than 30 springs along the Eleven Point. The Forest Service discourages drinking water from springs unless treated. Water from many springs is unsuitable. Among them, besides Greer, are Graveyard and Blue Spring, a large azure blue spring located at the Narrows part of the river. Caves of every size and description are to be found along the way.

To reach the River: If you decide to float the stream from Thomasville, take US 160 west from Poplar Bluff. If you decide to launch at Greer Spring, as many canoeists and floaters do because of the larger volume of water in the stream, take US 160 to Alton, then SR 19 north of Greer Spring.

WHERE TO DRIVE

Although this is not a river for cruising in an automobile, you can view certain portions of its beauty from several points. For instance, Greer Spring certainly can be reached by car and you might enjoy watching the flights of canoes and floaters taking off, usually early in the morning, as well as visiting the spring and the old mill.

US 160 crosses the Eleven Point at Riverton and two roads—Y and U—lead along the east and west sides of the stream to SR 142, some seven miles south. SR 142 crosses the Eleven Point near the Narrows and you can also visit Blue Spring from this point.

WHERE TO HIKE

Although a system of hiking trails are planned along the river, they are incomplete and hiking is limited. Since the situation changes periodically, it's best you check with the Forest Service just prior to planning a hiking expedition.

BACKPACKING OPPORTUNITIES

Like hiking, backpacking along the stream is limited, but back-packers are certainly welcome on portions of the trails that do exist. Camping is only at designated spots, principally at Greer Spring, McCormack Lake—just above Greer Spring—and at several float camps between Greer Springs and Riverton. The U.S. Forest Service publishes a map-brochure of the river indicating campsites and stream access points.

WHERE TO CAMP

Except for the points mentioned above, only a few private campgrounds are located in the area, however, some established campground are operated within a 50-mile radius in the Mark Twain National Forest. Consult the Forest Service for their locations.

Where to Obtain Information

Forest Supervisor
National Forests in Missouri
Box 937
Rolla, MO 65401

hercules glades wilderness

IN THE MARK Twain National Forest just 60 miles southeast of Springfield, Missouri, is the Hercules Glades Wilderness, comprising 16,648 acres. The area offers a variety of wild upland Ozark features including unusual scenery, open spaces with a feeling of remoteness, and a range of ecological zones. No permanent man-made installations are found here—just those created by nature.

It's an area mixed with open glades interspersed throughout a typical oak-hickory forest. Part of the area fronts on Bull Shoals Reservoir. Besides oak and hickory, red cedar is found over a large portion of the area. The open glades are covered with tall prairie grasses including big and little blue stem, Indian grass, switch grass, prairie dropseed and side oats grama, blackeyed susan, several species of corn flower, goldenrod and prairie clover. Hackberry, persimmon, cedar, and smoke trees are also found here.

Predominant features of the area are long narrow ridges with oc-

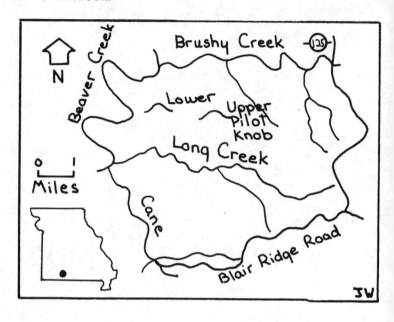

casional monadnocks or high knobs protruding above the skyline. And in between are the tall grass prairies. The entire drainage of Long Creek, which provides some most unusual rock formations, is within the area.

The climate here is generally humid with prevailing westerly winds. The area has year-around use, however, for the average January temperature is only about 25 degrees F. Thunderstorms of short duration in summer can cause flash flooding, so remember that when you pitch camp beside a stream or in a hollow surrounded by steep hills. Snow is infrequent.

Wildlife here includes coyote, bobcat, striped skunk, raccoon and opposum, red and gray fox, woodchuck and eastern cottontail rabbit, wild turkey, pileated woodpecker, grouse, copperhead, and rattlesnake.

To reach the area: From Springfield, take SR 125 south which leads right into this area.

WHERE TO DRIVE

The wilderness is bounded on the east by SR 125, on the south by Blair Ridge Road. These are all backroads with little traffic and you can wander along them at your own leisure enjoying the wilderness atmosphere at your fingertips. Be careful not to hit any wildlife as you travel these roads.

WHERE TO HIKE

While the terrain is generally rugged except for the open glades, you may find hiking here quite a pleasure during certain periods of the year. Fall, winter and spring are the best times to do it. No trails other than old logging roads exist in the area, but you may, by following along the stream drainage, make your own way into the area.

Only two hills of noteworthiness are located here—Lower and Upper Pilot Knob. For specific recommendations, contact the Recreation Officer of the National Forests in Missouri, at Rolla, Mo., for help in planning your hiking adventure.

BACKPACKING OPPORTUNITIES

Backpacking is permitted throughout the area, although it may be well to check in with the local Forest Ranger before going on an extensive jaunt. It's best to carry your own stove except during periods when the forestland is wet, for forest fires are a great problem in this part of the Ozarks. Be extremely careful. Carry a snakebite and first-aid kit.

WHERE TO CAMP

No established campgrounds are located within the area nor close by in the Mark Twain National Forest. But you can select a primitive camp anywhere you please in this wilderness. Just make sure you leave no signs of it's having been there when you leave. The key to a wilderness experience for those who come this way tomorrow is to keep it that way today. Because of the availability of water, you may find more choice places to camp along Long Creek.

Where to Obtain Information

Forest Supervisor
National Forests in Missouri
P.O. Box 937
Rolla, MO 65401

irish (whites creek) wilderness

IN OREGON COUNTY in southeast Missouri, as part of the Mark Twain National Forest, is located the Irish Wilderness Area with nearly 20,000 acres along the Eleven Point National, Scenic River. It bounds that river for seven miles. Although there's evidence of man's inroads here during past years, it's an impressive area with many karst features and rolling to steep hills ranging up to 900 feet tall.

Several short intermittent streams flow to the Eleven Point River. The valley of Whites Creek has several disappearing stream segments and small bluffs that expose the dolomitic sandstone and dolomite bedrock. One of the most significant karst features of the area is Whites Creek Cave, a spacious walk-in cavern with an entrance 20 feet wide and eight feet high. It leads some 900 feet into the hillside and can be explored without stooping. Stalactites, stalagmites, and flowstone are common crystalline formations in the cave. Also a number of smaller less impressive caves are located in the area.

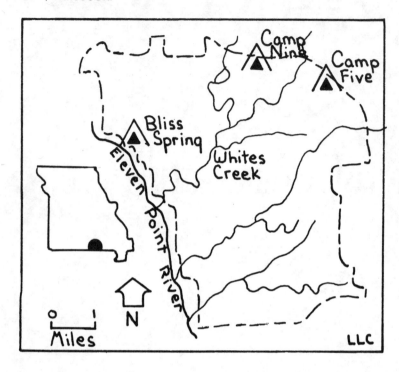

Since 1937, the Whites Creek or Irish area has been considered by the Forest Service as a special area and protected as that. Predominant trees are in the oak-hickory class with scattered shortleaf pine. In the river bottom silt-loam soils are black walnut, sycamore and prairie plants, along with eastern red cedar which stand in scattered open glades. Few giants are found here; most of the trees are 40 to 50 years old.

Wildlife is typical of the Missouri Ozarks including white-tailed deer, eastern wild turkey, gray squirrels, cottontail rabbits, raccoons, fox, coyotes, bobcats, beavers, rattlesnakes, and copperhead. Birds include the pileated woodpecker, owls, hawks, and an occasional bald eagle, although none are known to nest in the area.

To reach the area: From Alton take US 160 east and SH J north to Camp Five Pond. Forest Service Road 3228 and FS Road 3227 lead into the edge of the Irish wilderness.

WHERE TO DRIVE

The area is bounded on the north by Forest Service Road 4813 and Forest Service Road 3226, on the east by SR J, on the south by a part of Forest Service Road 3228. Or, if you are floating the Eleven Point Scenic Waterway, you can actually explore part of this wilderness from boat, as seven miles of it bounds the Irish Wilderness. All of these roads give the motorist a good get-acquainted tour with the area.

WHERE TO HIKE

A number of old logging roads plus some old railroad beds exist in the area and can be used for hiking. Some may present too dense undergrowth to be suitable; the hiker merely has to explore his own way and blaze his own trail, being always alert, of course, for copperheads or rattlers. In late fall, winter or early spring, the area is more open and conducive to hiking adventure.

Winters are normally mild with little snowfall. The Whites Creek Hiking Trail starts near Camp Five Pond and makes a grand sweep of the entire area to the Eleven Point River.

BACKPACKING OPPORTUNITIES

Although trails leave something to be desired, the area is good for backpacking the way pioneer Americans would have done it. Roughing it here is a worthwhile experience. Water is not plentiful, especially during extreme dry weather. It is better to take your own water. If springs are used, the water should be purified by boiling or chemically treated before using. Primitive camping is wherever you find it.

WHERE TO CAMP

Primitive camping may be done at any place one finds suitable or desirable in the area. An established picnic site is located at Camp Five Pond on the very northeastern perimeter of the area, reachable via FS Rd. 3226. Another site is at Camp Nine Pond, a pristine area nearby in the same vicinity. Water and pit toilets are available at both.

Where to Obtain Information

Forest Supervisor
National Forests in Missouri
P.O. Box 937
Rolla, MO 65401

NEBRASKA

crescent lake wilderness

IN THE SOUTHWESTERN corner of the great sandhills region of Nebraska is the Crescent Lake Wilderness, a part of the Crescent Lake National Wildlife Refuge, just 26 miles from Oshkosh. The sand hills are aged dunes protected from wind erosion by a thin covering of grasses and forbs. Shallow lakes, marshes, and grassy meadows are found between the ridges and hills, and dune configurations are variable, from gently rolling to high, abruptly-sloped ranges several miles long. The highest dunes with the steepest slopes are called "choppies." Some are as high as 200 feet.

The area is one of the most unique ecosystems in all of America which makes it a most unusual wilderness. This is, for instance, the world's only sizable sand dune area not a desert. Grasses are sustained by precipitation ranging from 16 to 24 inches annually, yet underground is a vast reservoir estimated to be in excess of 700-million acre-feet of fresh water. Grass cover is mostly sand

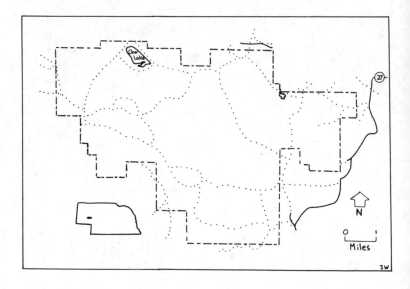

reedgrass, sand bluestem, sand lovegrass, switchgrass and hairy gramma. Blowout grass is the first species to establish itself on eroded sands and is commonly succeeded by sandhill muhley. Other growth includes spiderwort, prairie sage, skeleton weed, sand psoralea and ragweed, sunflower, sand spurge, and narrow-leaved lambsquarter. Yucca and prickly pear cactus are common on hillsides. Sand cherry and prairie rose are also found spotted throughout the area, while in wet areas are cottonwood, American elm, almond-leaf willow, ash, hackberry, choke cherry and wild plum.

Climate is hot and dry with temperatures often exceeding 100 degrees during July and August; in winter heavy snows and blizzards make life nearly unbearable. Of the 46,000 acres in the refuge, approximately 24,500 are considered appropriate for a wilderness experience.

Wildlife found here includes antelope, white-tailed and mule deer, kangaroo rats, coyotes, badger, three species of rabbits including jackrabbits, raccoon, pheasant, mink and muskrat, snapping turtle, painted turtle, watersnake and the bullsnake. Fish include bluegill, largemouth bass, northern pike, carp, yellow perch, and bullhead. No fishing lakes, however, are located within the wilderness; they're in the adjacent wildlife refuge.

This is one of the most uncrowded wilderness areas in America, normally attracting less than 2,000 people annually. Wildlife observation, hunting, fishing, bird watching and hiking are primary pastimes.

To reach the area: From Oshkosh take SR 27 north to the refuge. US 26 runs east-west through Oshkosh and intersects with SR 27.

WHERE TO DRIVE

Roads are scarce in this part of Nebraska where the terrain becomes of pronounced western appearance. Only one road of consequence leads through the refuge and that's a four and a half mile section of a north-south country road—an extension of SR 27. It's a poor quality oil mat.

Other roads on the western portion of the refuge are unsurfaced and only partially graded, but can be driven. They're dusty, but if you want to experience wilderness or gather in the atmosphere of this land, you won't mind the dust—it's a part of it. Check with the refuge headquarters before taking your motor jaunt, however. Personnel there can advise you on the best places to see wildlife along the way.

WHERE TO HIKE

More than 50 miles of sand trails exist in the wilderness area, but the terrain here is such that you may choose your own path across the sand hills. Your only concern need be for the fragile vegetation covering the area. Several small potholes for wildlife watering spots are located in the wilderness and these are good places to spot wildlife, particularly during the early morning or late afternoon. You'll likely want to carry your own drinking water.

BACKPACKING OPPORTUNITIES

Backpacking is permitted, but limited because of the fragile conditions of the terrain. You should carry water because of the hot, arid climate. There's no camping permitted anywhere on the refuge.

WHERE TO CAMP

No camping is permitted on the refuge but there are a couple of state-operated campgrounds near Ogallala on US 26, some 40 miles east of Oshkosh, and another near Bridgeport on US 26, several miles to the west. All are state recreation areas.

Where to Obtain Information

Refuge Manager
Crescent Lake Nat'l Wildlife Refuge
Ellsworth, NE 69340

valentine national wildlife refuge

ON THE VALENTINE National Wildlife Refuge in the sandhills of north central Nebraska is a 16,317-acre tract the prairie chicken has called home for many years. The terrain here is a series of sandhill ranges called "choppies," locally, with smooth valleys between the ranges. In the lowest valleys are lakes with surfaces slightly above the water table. Tree growth is limited to the shores of these lakes; the remainder of the area is covered with a sparse grass. Because erosion could be a problem here, no hiking trails will be built, but the terrain is such that you don't need a trail; just strike out cross-country after charting your course.

The lakes and marshy areas in the valleys are attractive spots for wildlife, and waterfowl are found here. Two large lakes—Dad's and Mule—are included in the wilderness section in addition to a number of small ones. The smaller lakes are entirely surrounded by marshes. Rare species of wildlife found here include the peregrine falcon, greater sandhill crane, greater prairie chicken, bald eagle,

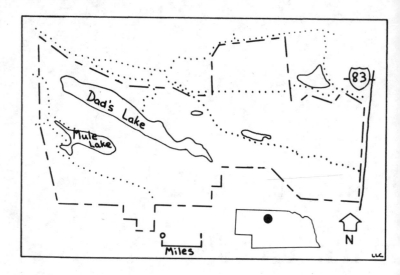

golden eagle, and trumpeter swan. Other types of wildlife include the long-billed curlew, mule and white-tailed deer, coyote, white-tailed jackrabbit, muskrat, raccoon, red fox, stripped skunk, rattlesnake, and Canada geese. During migration periods, a number of species of ducks are also here.

To reach the area: Take US 83 south from the town of Valentine. It divides the wildlife refuge and is directly bordering the wilderness.

WHERE TO DRIVE

US 83, which has generally light traffic, borders the eastern portion of the area. A gravel road leads along portions of the northern boundary, across Calf Camp Marsh and School Lake. This is an excellent route from which to view the area and watch the wildlife.

WHERE TO HIKE

Because erosion from wind is such a great problem on the sparsely-vegetated fine sand terrain, trails are seldom established here and hikers are asked not to walk single file, but abreast, so as not to create trails. A few public access trails have been built, one of them leading to Dad's Lake, another from Coleman Lake on the southern border to Mule Lake. Other trails lead out of the area and onto portions of the wildlife refuge. Fishing is a great sport here and many come not only to hike, but to fish the lakes for largemouth bass, crappie, and brim.

BACKPACKING OPPORTUNITIES

Although overnight camping is not permitted on the refuge, backpackers are welcome. It is difficult walking on the sand, however, and for that reason plus the temperature extremes, it is not a popular backpacking area. Water is plentiful, but must be treated by boiling or chemical additives before drinking. Shade is only found along the lakes and then only sparsely. The hazard of sunstroke is something to be considered during warm-weather hiking. Be sure to take along snakebite and first-aid kits as well as some water when hiking here.

WHERE TO CAMP

No camping is permitted here, but there is camping available near the town of Valentine in private campgrounds. Check with its Chamber of Commerce for details.

Where to Obtain Information

Refuge Manager
Fort Niobrara, Valentine Nat'l Wildlife Refuge
Hidden Timber Route
Valentine, NE 69201

Chamber of Commerce
Valentine, NE 69201

KENTUCKY

beaver creek wilderness

IN KENTUCKY'S APPALACHIA foothills is a scenic sunken canyon wilderness. Consisting of 5,000 acres in the Daniel Boone National Forest, the area is surrounded by large sandstone cliffs in the Beaver Creek watershed. Irregularly shaped, it ranges some five miles long and up to about three miles wide. In the upper portion of the drainage, the cliffs are nearly continuous. Many rock houses and shallow caves pockmark the area.

The entire region is underlain with interbedded sequences of sandstone and shale. The beds have been eroded by streams to form maturely dissected, irregular land surfaces with winding ridges and narrow steep-sided valleys. Some of the cliffs rise from 200 to 400 feet. Beaver Creek drains into Lake Cumberland. The climate here is generally pleasant with an extreme range from about five to 100 degrees. Rainfall averages about 46 inches annually.

The area is usable year-around and winter backpacking is as

A pause for the view while hiking in the Beaver Creek Wilderness, Kentucky

pleasant as in summer. Most rainfall occurs during the spring season—March through May. Snowfall occurs from December through March, but normally does not stay on the ground more than two to three days. Vegetation consists of mixed pine, hemlock, maple, elm, ash, yellow poplar, various oaks and hickory. Rhododendron and mountain laurel also are found here.

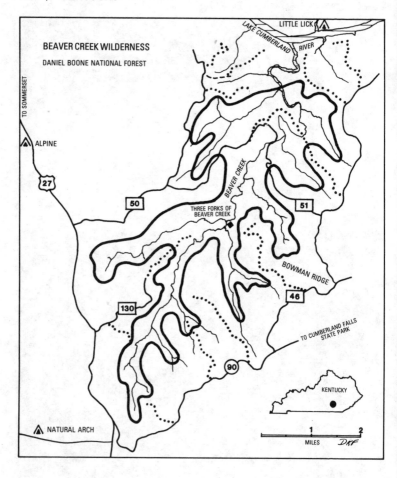

Wildlife includes ruffed grouse, wild turkey, white-tailed deer and bobcat together with a multitude of smaller animals and birds. Occasionally a bald eagle is spotted but no nesting occurs here.

To reach the area: Take US 27 south from Somerset to the wilderness area. Obtain a Forest Service map from the District Ranger station in Somerset prior to going to the area.

WHERE TO DRIVE

Roads lead around much of the wilderness area. On the upper end of the watershed, Forest Service Road 130 leads a short distance into the wilderness from the end of which begins a short trail leading across Hurricane Creek. No roads except the end of FS 130 provide an opportunity to view the wilderness area from your automobile.

WHERE TO HIKE

The area has two trails. One follows Beaver Creek and is primarily used by fishermen. The other starts on Bowman Ridge and leads to the overlook of Three Forks of Beaver Creek, a distance of about a mile, one of the most spectacular overlooks in this portion of the Daniel Boone National Forest.

BACKPACKING OPPORTUNITIES

Backpackers are welcome on the trails or to strike out cross-country for that matter. Although no campsites are established, many possible sites exist near the trail. The Bowman Ridge Trail has a small brook nearby; the other runs along Beaver Creek providing an ample supply of water and some fine fishing for bluegill, smallmouth bass, and trout. Be sure to boil or chemically treat the water before using. Pack out all litter and garbage.

WHERE TO CAMP

No established campsites are available, but you may choose your own site at any place in the wilderness area. Other established campsites are available within 25 miles in the Daniel Boone National Forest or at Cumberland Falls State Park. No cutting of live material is permitted on Forest Service land, but you can use downed dead wood.

Where to Obtain Information

District Ranger
U.S. Forest Service
Somerset, KY 42501

Supervisor
Daniel Boone Nat'l Forest
Winchester, KY 40391

cumberland gap wilderness

LOCATED IN THE passage of the Appalachians connecting Kentucky, Tennessee, and Virginia lies Cumberland Gap National Historical Park, containing more than 21,000 acres of mountain wilderness. Cumberland Gap itself is a notch in Cumberland Mountain that was much used by Indian war parties and hunting parties and later by a mass migration of colonists to Kentucky and the West. On park lands in the vicinity of the gap are two miles of the original Wilderness Road blazed by Daniel Boone in 1775. Other predominant features include the Pinnacle with a magnificent view of the surrounding sountry, Cudjo Cave (privately operated) and Tri-State Park where the three states meet.

These are exceedingly rugged mountains with precipitous slopes forming cliffs in many places, some of the highest being the White Rocks viewed from Virginia. As viewed from Powell Valley, the south face of Cumberland Mountain and the famous White Rock cliffs look very much as they did when the early pioneers trekked

(U.S. Department of the Interior, National Park Service Photo)
A view of Chimney Rock in the Cumberland Gap Wilderness, Kentucky

through Cumberland Gap. Flora includes predominantly oak, hickory, a variety of evergreens including pines, hemlock, American holly, rhododendron, and mountain laurel. Redbud and dogwood trees color the landscape in spring.

Wildlife includes ruffed grouse, turkey vulture, numerous species of hawks and owls, occasional bald eagle, rabbit, fox, raccoons, possums, bobcat, and white-tailed deer. Geologically, the region has

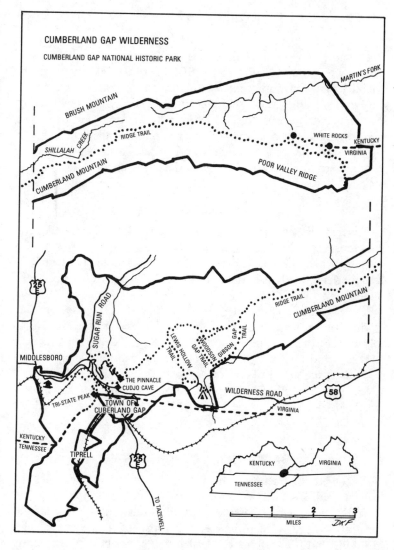

been subjected to great earth stresses, producing folded and faulted rocks.

To reach the park: From Middlesboro, Kentucky, take US 25E south the the visitors' center. From Tazewell, Tennessee, take US 25 E north.

WHERE TO DRIVE

Short portions of US 25 and US 58 pass through one end of the park and that's about as close to the wilderness as you can get by automobile. Sugar Run Road (SR 988) runs north from the vicinity of the visitors' center and gives one a feeling for the park and its wilderness. Off US 58 five miles east of the visitors' center is a short loop road which also allows one to experience a limited amount of wilderness. However, hiking trails lead from this area. From the visitors' center you can take a four-mile drive to the Pinnacle for a bird's eye view of the entire countryside.

WHERE TO HIKE

Several extensive trails lead through this wilderness. The longest and most rugged is Ridge Trail, 21 miles long. The shortest trail is less than a mile. The Ridge Trail leads right along the crest of Cumberland, the Brush Mountains—on one side is Virginia, on the other Kentucky.

Other trails include the Lewis Hollow Trail, Woodson Gap Trail, Gibson Gap Trail, the short Wilderness Trail leading to an old Iron Furnace, a trail leading up Tri-State Peak from 25E near the gap, and the Skylight Cave Trail. You can hike along a short section of the famous Wilderness Road, the same trail that Daniel Boone built. A hiker's guide to Cumberland Gap called *Boot and Blister* is published by the National Park Service and is available from the visitors' center.

BACKPACKING OPPORTUNITIES

Excellent for backpacking. The complex of trails includes excellent challenges in the high country for those who would experience this wilderness. Water is plentiful through most of the area as several streams bisect the region. Most of it is suitable for drinking, but it is recommended that you either boil or chemically treat it first.

WHERE TO CAMP

Camping is available at the Wilderness Road Campground and in the backcountry at Martins Fork Cabin and campsites. No other camping is permitted. Camping permits are required for camping at Martins Fork. During periods of high fire danger, "no smoking" signs will be posted throughout the trail system and this regulation will be strictly enforced.

Reservations for the Martins Fork Cabin and the campsites at Martins Fork are available on a first-come, first-served basis and may be made in person by writing Cumberland Gap National Historical Park. The Wilderness Road Campground contains 165 sites. Programs are presented nightly in the amphitheater during the summer months. A picnic area is located nearby.

Where to Obtain Information

Superintendent
Cumberland Gap Nat'l Historical Park
P.O. Box 840
Middlesboro, KY 40965

lilley cornett woods

IN THE APPALACHIAN foothills of southeastern Kentucky is located the largest known remnant of one of the greatest forests of all time—the Mixed Mesophytic Forest. Called the Lilley Cornett Woods, with an area of 554 acres much of which is virgin timber, it contains more species of trees than any other forest in the world outside the tropics. A few mountain areas in China may contain a similar forest and a few small tracts elsewhere may contain some traces of this era.

At least 64 species of trees have been identified here, many of them growing when Columbus discovered America. Many are giants—a red oak more than 51 inches in diameter and 150 feet tall, a chestnut oak 47 plus inches in diameter. Many of the plants growing in the woods are rarely found elsewhere—crested dwarf iris, pink lady's slipper, spotted mandarin, belleart and some species of trillium.

Giant hemlocks reaching for the sky form a cathedral ceiling over

The Lilley Cornett Woods in Kentucky is noted for its variety of trees.

rocks and wild flowers here creating a most desirable wilderness atmosphere, survival of these trees is due to the late Lilley Cornett's intense devotion to the woods. After working all week in the coal mines, he would often take his family into the woods for a picnic lunch on Sundays. During heavy fire danger, he would pay crews out of his own pocket to go into the woods and protect them.

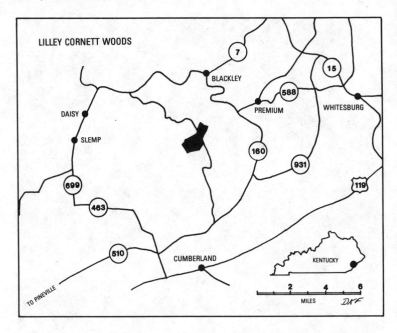

He constantly refused to allow any logging operations in the woods; only the huge chestnuts killed by blight were cut.

The heirs to the property transferred title to the Commonwealth of Kentucky in 1969 so the woods could be permanently preserved for posterity.

To reach the Woods: From Whitesburg, take SR 15 north to Isom, then pick up SR 7 to SR 1103 north which leads directly to the woods.

WHERE TO DRIVE

KY Route 1103 leads directly through the woods and that's about the extent of experiencing this woodland by automobile. Park in the parking lot and take a guided tour provided by a state forester.

WHERE TO HIKE

Only a limited number of persons are allowed in the woods at a single time, and only on guided tours, 9 a.m. to 4:30 p.m. daily, November to March. Drop a postcard or call in advance.

BACKPACKING OPPORTUNITIES

Because this forest is so small and so rare, no backpacking is permitted.

WHERE TO CAMP

Although no camping is permitted at the Lilley Cornett Woods, nearby Kingdom Come State Park, Pine Mountain State Resort Park at Pineville, and Cumberland Gap National Historical Park at Middlesboro offer established and primitive campsites. To the east are Fishtrap Lake and Breaks Interstate Park and to the west Buckhorn Lake State Resort Park and the Redbird Purchase Area of the Daniel Boone National Forest, all of which offer hiking and camping opportunities.

Where to Obtain Information

Superintendent
Lilley Cornett Woods
Skyline, KY 41851

Director
Division of Forestry
Frankfort, KY 40601

mammoth cave wilderness

AT MAMMOTH CAVE National Park in south central Kentucky lies an underground wilderness, probably the most extensive in North America. In almost all areas of the park south of the Green River are important underground features. Flint Ridge, a large area to the north and northeast of Mammoth Cave is believed to be the longest cave system in the world. Flint Ridge Cave System was linked to Mammoth Cave with the discovery of a connecting passage in September, 1972.

It is the longest cave system in the world. Present surveyed mileage is 165-170 miles. A great deal of the system remains largely unexplored. This portion had not been opened to the public, only to scientific and educational institutions. Visitors are not permitted to enter any cave on their own. The Flint Ridge System is not open to public use at this time.

Directly south of the Mammoth Cave visitor complex is the Jim Lee Ridge and to its west Joppa Ridge, constituting a region of karst

(Courtesy, American Airlines)
Scene during a cave tour, Mammoth Cave, Kentucky

believed to cover a third major cave system. The areas under Flint, Joppa and Jim Lee Ridges can be considered a subterranean wilderness. The major source of water for the cave system of Flint Ridge is the percolation from surface springs that have been capped to provide water for the lodge and campgrounds in the national park

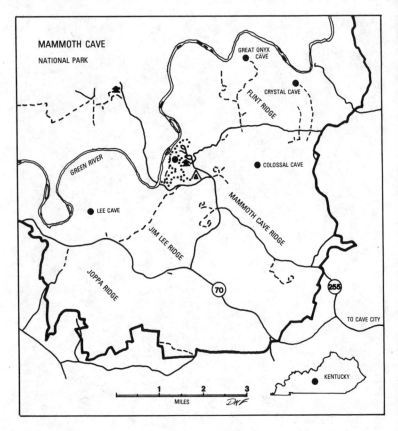

and also water that flows through subterranean conduits from the sinkhole plain.

A wild cave tour is offered by the National Park Service in one section of Mammoth Cave. This constitutes a most dramatic spelunking experience, but only for the physically fit. The Wild Cave Tour is restricted to 15 persons accompanied by a park guide. Each spulunker is provided with a pair of knee pads and a yellow helmet with a battery-powered light. Packrats make their home in this part of the cave and you may see some of them. Bruised shins and battered egos are part of this experience, but once you've completed it, you'll have a greater understanding of a most unique type of wilderness.

To reach the Cave: Take I-65 south from Louisville to the towns of Cave City or Park City. Exits here lead west to Mammoth Cave National Park where you may inquire at the headquarters for directions to the wild cave tour.

BACKPACKING OPPORTUNITIES

No backpacking or overnight use is permitted in the cave, but you may backpack topside on some of the trails in the national park which are not wilderness, but offer solitude and an opportunity to escape the crowds.

WHERE TO CAMP

Campgrounds are located in the national park and a number of privately-operated campgrounds including two KOA's are located nearby. You may also camp in established campgrounds in the park, but the experience does not qualify as wilderness.

Where to Obtain Information

Park Superintendent
Mammoth Cave Nat'l Park
Mammoth Cave, KY 42259

bowater pocket wilderness

THE LAUREL-SNOW Pocket Wilderness is the largest of several pocket wilderness areas set aside for public use by Bowater in the South. Comprising 710 acres, it includes two impressive waterfalls—Laurel and Snow Falls, pristine sections of Laurel, Morgan and Richland creeks, part of a gulf and a stand of virgin timber. Geological formations include natural rockhouses or shallow caves. Shortleaf pine, yellow poplar, oaks, dogwood and other mountain trees cover the rugged hills and valleys where raccoon, red fox, and white-tailed deer roam. While small, the area is rugged and provides a challenging wilderness experience.

To reach the area: From Dayton take US 27 north, turn west at Rhea County Hospital and follow signs two miles to entrance.

Not the largest waterfall in Tennessee, but one of the most beautiful—Snow Falls in Bowater Pocket Wilderness

WHERE TO DRIVE

Aside from the drive to the parking area at the entrance to the wilderness, there are no driving opportunities here.

WHERE TO HIKE

A single trail leads into the wilderness from the parking area and ultimately splits with branches leading to Laurel Falls and

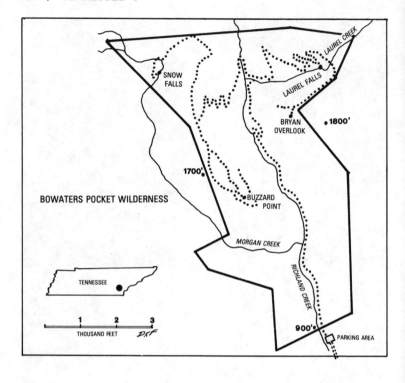

Snow Falls. These branches also include Buzzard Point and Bryan Overlook. A large portion of the trail leads along Richland Creek from which you usually may use the water except after heavy rains, provided you treat it chemically.

The complete round-trip hike to both waterfalls is about eight miles long and includes two climbs and descents of about 900 feet, providing a good eight-hour hike. Use special caution around overlooks where cliffs are more than 100 feet high. The Laurel-Snow Trail was the first one in Tennessee to be designated by the Bureau of Outdoor Recreation and Department of Interior as a National Recreation Trail.

BACKPACKING OPPORTUNITIES

The company prefers that camping be confined to the general parking area, or that a company-maintained primitive camp at Spring City, 15 miles to the north, be used as a base. Overuse could damage the Pocket Wilderness area.

WHERE TO CAMP

Primitive camping only.

Where to Obtain Information

Public Relations Dept.
Bowaters Southern Paper Corp.
Calhoun, TN 37309

(Note: The Bowater also has established smaller wilderness areas in Tennessee and North Carolina, all with hiking trails.)

gee creek wilderness

IN SOUTHEASTERN TENNESSEE'S Polk County is the Gee Creek Wilderness, embodying 1,069 acres of cascades and waterfalls on a pristine stream through a rugged gorge. Bounded on each side by steep ridges and unbroken vegetation including pockets of huge old trees, this is one of the most impressive of the "new" wilderness areas. Opportunities for solitude and enjoyment of esthetic amenities are excellent.

Gee Creek runs cold and clear with deep holes where lurk great rainbow trout. Present are white-tailed deer, turkey, ruffed grouse, fox, European wild boar, raccoon, opossum, groundhogs, and cottontail rabbits. The trout here are wild. Located in the Cherokee National Forest, Gee Creek passes through a deep gorge between Starr Mountain and Chestnut Mountain, an area of sharp relief with elevations ranging 1,000 to 2,500 feet above sea level. Steep slopes with rock outcrops along the gorge are common. The creek drops 700 feet through the gorge with numerous waterfalls and cascades, some

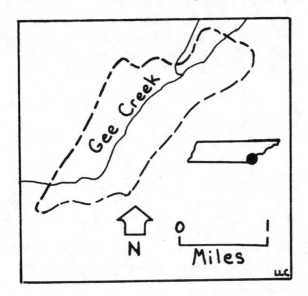

ranging from five to 20 feet in height. The upper water depths range from 4-8 inches deep.

The woodland contains white oak, red oak, northern red oak, yellow poplar, hickory, shortleaf and Virginia pines, underscored with a large variety of native flowers, ferns and shrubs. Average rainfall here ranges up to 55 inches annually with four to six inches of snow. Mean temperatures range from around 40 in January to 76 in July. The entire area is rugged mountainous terrain, lying at the western edge of the Blue Ridge Mountains.

To reach the Wilderness: From Etowah, Tennessee, take US 411 south and turn east on an unnumbered gravel road along the north side of Hiwassee River. After crossing Gee Creek, turn north to the area.

WHERE TO DRIVE

SR 30 leading along the Hiwassee River gives the motorist a good idea of what the area is like and provides an excellent outdoor scenic experience. But it is not wilderness. To sample Gee

Creek, one may drive to the boundaries, park and walk into the area. A gravel road—Forest Service Road 297-1, leads along a portion of the northern boundary. Check with the headquarters of the Cherokee National Forest or the District Ranger for further details.

WHERE TO HIKE

Trails into the area are quite limited. One of the most popular is a trail leading from the vicinity of Iron Gap, paralleling Gee Creek for a short distance and then cutting west again. Another follows the crest of Chestnut Mountain. Most of the area remains trailess for those who wish to create their own adventure by exploring new paths through this wilderness, much as early explorers did.

BACKPACKING OPPORTUNITIES

Backpacking is excellent and there's an ample water supply. There are plenty of primitive spots to camp. Just make sure you keep it that way, and upon departure leave no trace of your campsite. Many backpackers into this area like to combine their experience with fishing for wild rainbow trout. Beware: Rattlesnakes and copperheads also occupy this wilderness. Be sure to take along a snakebite and first-aid kit.

WHERE TO CAMP

No established campsites are located in the area. Make your own. There are some established campgrounds within an hour's drive in the Cherokee National Forest, including a KOA campground and the Quina Springs Recreation Area nearby, if you prefer to camp there. Check with the Forest Supervisor for locations and details.

Where to Obtain Information

Forest Supervisor
Cherokee Nat'l Forest
U.S. Forest Service, P.O. Box 400
Cleveland, TN 37311

District Ranger
P.O. Box 349
Etowah, TN 37311

great smoky mountains

THE GREAT SMOKY Mountains area is America's most popular national park, but one need only turn away from the beaten paths to find an abundance of wilderness and a fantastic wilderness experience. Once you're out of earshot of traffic on the busy roads leading through the park, you've found your niche in a world that offers serenity and seclusion, rugged beauty and an abundance of wildlife. Forming the boundary between North Carolina and Tennessee, the Smokies are a majestic climax to the Appalachian Highlands.

One may stand atop a mountain and count the ridge outlines faintly etched before him as far as the eye can see, outlines softened by a dense mantle of forestland that swishes away in sweeping troughs and mighty billows. The name, incidentally, is derived from the blue smoke-like haze that envelopes these mountains. Containing virtually an unspoiled forest much akin to that found by early pioneers who happened this way, the park is a wil-

(Travel Information Division, Department of
Conservation and Development, North Carolina)

Fishing Soco Creek, Great Smoky Mountains, Tennessee

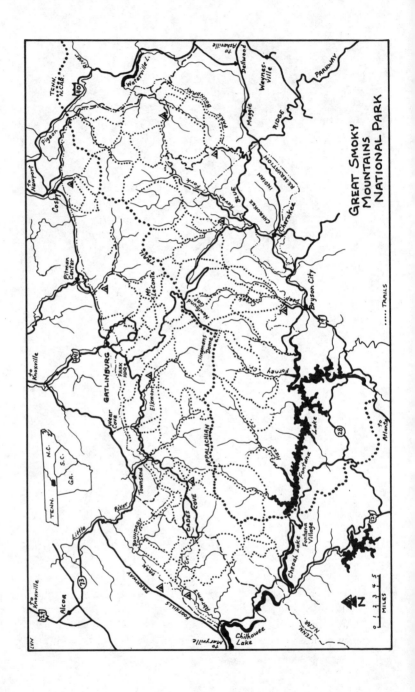

GREAT SMOKY MOUNTAINS NATIONAL PARK

derness sanctuary for both plants and animals. Fertile soils and heavy rains over a long period have created a veritable rainforest with more than 1,400 kinds of flowering plants. Within the coves, broadleaf trees predominate while along the crest of the ridges, some rising as high as 6,000 feet, conifer forests such as those of Ontario, Canada, prevail.

Between the mountains are rushing trout streams, providing picturesque vistas. Many are habitat for brook, brown and rainbow trout. You may fish year-around but better do it on a fish-for-fun basis only. Only those larger than 16 inches may be kept under Park Service regulations. And that's rare in a stream trout here.

Wildlife includes black bear, white-tailed deer, bobcat, raccoon, pileated woodpecker, bald eagle and a variety of smaller animals and birds. Wildflowers bloom profusely beginning in February throughout the summer. The most colorful time is March, April and May, however.

To reach the park: From Gatlinburg, take SR 73 south to the Park Headquarters and Visitor Center where you may obtain maps and literature as well as recommendations from park service personnel to make your stay more meaningful.

WHERE TO DRIVE

Most of the people who come to the Smokies enjoy it from their automobile. A road system leads through much of the park to allow motorists a look at unspoiled beauty. The main roads, of course, offer only an introduction to the park.

At Cades Cove an 11-mile loop auto tour leads past open fields, pioneer homesteads and little clapboard country churches where mountain people lived and worshipped almost unnoticed for more than a century. A scenic high mountain road leads through Newfound Gap to Clingmans Dome where you can take a half-mile walk to an observation tower. Remember to drive slowly and carefully, for park roads were not built for speed but instead for enjoyment.

In Gatlinburg is a motor nature trail leading into the park, one of the most interesting drives in the Smokies. Although it includes only a few miles, one can actually spend a full day on this auto nature trail alone. Short walks off this trail lead to Grotto Falls and Rainbow Falls. Not in the park, but close by the western boundary is the Foothills Parkway, maintained by the Park Service. Here is one of the most spectacular drives of the Smokies! Don't miss it.

WHERE TO HIKE

Many many hiking trails exist in the Smokies. More than 25 are considered favorite hiking trails, ranging from one-quarter mile to 15 miles in length. The Appalachian Trail leads through the center of the Great Smoky Mountains, following generally the main crestline. A booklet called *Hiking in the Great Smokies* by Carson Brewer is a fine guide to the trails and is available at the visitors' center.

Many of the trails lead to scenic points such as waterfalls, vistas and some lead along roaring pristine streams. One could, in fact, spend several months hiking all the trails in the Smokies without covering the same ground twice. The Park Service also publishes a list of the most popular hiking trails in the park, which you might write to get before going there.

BACKPACKING OPPORTUNITIES

The Smokies probably affords the greatest backpacking opportunities in the eastern wilderness. Because of the great complex of trails, the numerous streams bisecting the area, the rugged challenge and beauty of the terrain and seclusion of primitive campsites, thousands of backpackers come here annually to experience this bit of wilderness. Climate is generally mild enough for use ten months of the year and even snow backpacking is becoming more and more popular. Rangers check your clothing and equipment during snow months, however, to insure your safety while in the mountains.

WHERE TO CAMP

Choose your own campsite from the numerous designated camping areas found along the trails. Shelters which are available on a reservation basis only are spaced periodically along the Appalachian Trail. Also there are seven developed campgrounds in the park. Beware of leaving food which will attract bears. If on the trail, tie your food up into a tree which helps avoid detection by bears. Keep no garbage around your tentsite.

Where to Obtain Information

Superintendent
Great Smoky Mountains Nat'l Park
Gatlinburg, TN 37738

ARKANSAS

caney creek backcountry

CONSISTING OF 10,236 pristine acres, this backcountry has clear streams, picturesque rock outcroppings and sharp ridges with sweeping vistas. A part of a 100,000 game management unit administered by the Arkansas Game and Fish Commission, the Caney Creek Backcountry is part of the Ouachita National Forest.

Openings created to provide food for wildlife are designed so they blend into the landscape as do natural forest openings. These wildlife plots are heavily used and hikers often can see a variety of wild birds and animals at fairly close range . . . white-tailed deer, turkey, black bear and squirrels, plus many other small animals, birds, and reptiles.

The streams provide good fishing for smallmouth bass, longear and green sunfish, rock bass, and spotted black bass. Be sure to keep a sharp eye out for copperheads and rattlesnakes. It's a good idea to carry a snakebite kit with you at all times.

In 1935, President Franklin Roosevelt set aside 8,300 acres as the

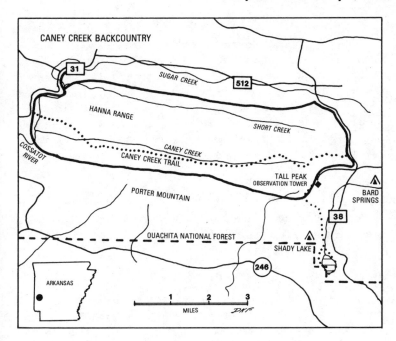

Caney Creek Wildlife Refuge and in 1968 it was re-established as the Caney Creek Game Management unit. Views from the ridgetops include panoramas of pine-clad flatlands to the south and continuous rows of east-west tree-clad ridges to the north, east, and west. Nearby mountain ridges exhibit numerous broken sandstone bluffs.

To reach the area: From Hot Springs, take US 70 to SR 84, then FS Road 38 which leads directly past the Caney Creek Back-country.

WHERE TO DRIVE

Forest Service Road 38, 31 and 512 border on three sides of the area, thus giving the motorist ample opportunity to survey the terrain and general atmosphere. A drive-to campground is located nearby at Bard Springs.

WHERE TO HIKE

Two principal trails lead into or through the Caney Creek Backcountry. One main one is the Caney Creek Trail, nine miles long, extending along the creek from one end of the wilderness area to the other. It connects Forest Services Roads 38 and 31 and crosses the creek several times, so be prepared to wade or become a broad jumper. The other trail is two and a half miles long connecting Shady Lake south of the wilderness area to Tall Fire Tower overlooking Caney Creek Backcountry.

BACKPACKING OPPORTUNITIES

Prime backpacking country. Many have used it for years and you'll find many campsites used previously.

WHERE TO CAMP

Camping is open; choose your own site, but make sure to leave nothing and do not disturb the wilderness environment. Established campgrounds are located nearby at Bard Springs just east of Caney Creek and at Shady Lake just south of it. Campers be particularly careful with fires as this is a high-risk area.

Where to Obtain Information

Forest Supervisor
Ouachita Nat'l Forest
Hot Springs, AR 71901

District Ranger
U.S. Forest Service
Mena, AR 71953

OKLAHOMA

glover river wilderness

IN SOUTHEASTERN OKLAHOMA is the Glover River, not a
designated wilderness, but its nature is enough to provide an excellent wilderness experience by canoe or small boat for some 45
miles. Much of that distance, the Glover runs through rough hill
country of the southern Ouachitas.

The upper Glover is colorful and scenic, flowing often over solid
bedrock with many boulders along the banks and in and under the
water. Many natural dams—up-tilted hardrock ledges across the
river—cause the water to spill and tumble down noisy falls and
cascades. When the river is low, those ledges or natural dams have
to be portaged. At normal level, most of the rapids and cascades
can be navigated. When the river is above normal or near flood
stage, stay off. The falls then can be treacherous.

All along this section, the hill country has a strong flavor of wilderness with mile upon mile of unbroken forest. Picturesque pines
stand on the high places. Rocky outcrops and bluffs, gray-green

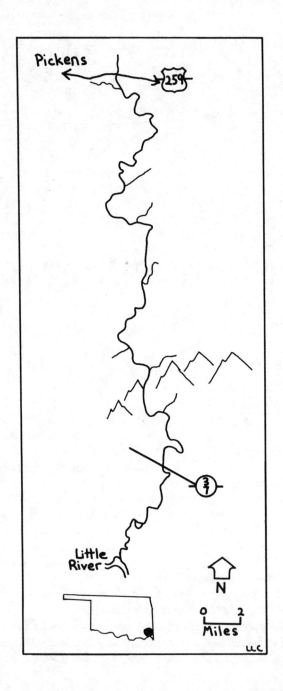

Pickens

259

Little
River

N

0   2
Miles

LLC

with lichens, overlook the stream. A jungle of vegetation crowds close to the banks. In spring, dogwood and redbud brighten the landscape with splashes of bloom.

From Mile 32, the river takes on a different look, running past lowland forest and cleared pastures. The bottom of the stream is now most often gravel or sand. Only a few springs are found along the river; so take your own water or something with which to purify it. Some floaters, particularly the area residents, say it's pure enough to drink and they do it directly from the stream.

Most of the unfenced or posted land along the Glover belongs to the Weyerhauser Company and their land remains open for public use as long as it is not abused by littering, etc. Stay off fenced land.

Normally the best time to float the Glover is from March to mid-June and from mid-September to mid-November. This depends upon weather and the type of season, however.

The upper parts of the river where rocks and rapids are too numerous to count, is not an easy float except for someone who's used to it. But experienced canoeists can do it with no difficulty if they take the trouble to study the river beforehand. Scout your rapids, if in doubt, before you attempt to run them, and then decide if you need to portage.

You may see considerable wildlife along the stream including white-tailed deer coming to drink, mink, raccoon, hawks, turkey vultures, owls—also a great variety of songbirds, perhaps even a bobcat.

To reach the River: From Broken Bow, take US 259 north to SR 144, then the road to Pickens. Once you've passed through a little village named Battiest, you'll soon cross the Glover at Mile 0 and the place to launch. Several other roads cross the Glover at various points along the way including SRs 3 and 7 near North Pole. For other recommendations, contact Jim Jones, 501 East Craig, Broken Bow, OK 74728.

WHERE TO DRIVE

Naturally you can drive through the Glover River country, but that isn't going to give you a wilderness experience. Several roads lead either adjacent or to the Glover at various points. If you take

SR 3 west from Broken Bow and turn right on the first road past the bridge over the Glover River at North Pole, you'll be able to see some of the river country. Other roads further along the way include Wolf Hollow, Meat Hollow, and Bear Mountain. But it's best to talk to residents at the towns of North Pole, Bethel or Battiest for their recommendations on where to drive in the area.

WHERE TO HIKE

Hiking cross-country is difficult because of the dense vegetation, but several old logging roads and some new ones have been constructed on land belonging to Weyerhauser Paper Co., and the public is welcome to use them as hiking trails. Best source of information on the old trails or logging roads is the U.S. Geological Survey maps (15-minute quads for Bethel and Golden). They're available from the Map Distribution Section, US Geological Survey, Federal Center, Denver, Colo., 80225.

WHERE TO CANOE

From Mile 0 near Battiest down to the ridge on SR 3 and 7 near North Pole is the greatest section of the Glover to float during normal water levels. You can do it yourself or contact Jim Jones (address listed earlier, this section) who is a canoe and fishing guide on this river.

BACKPACKING OPPORTUNITIES

Backpacking is permitted on Weyerhauser lands along the old logging roads provided you leave no trace of having been there. But check with any of the Weyerhauser local offices for permission before doing so. Their address is: The Craig Plant, Broken Bow, OK 74728.

WHERE TO CAMP

Campsites are all along the stream (all primitive) on sand and gravel bars or along the shaded banks. You also may camp along the old logging roads, but be sure to carry away all litter. No organized campgrounds are located in the area.

Where to Obtain Information

Jim Jones
501 East Craig
Broken Bow, OK 74728

Dept. of Wildlife Conservation
1801 N. Lincoln
Oklahoma City, OK 73105

m_cCurtain county
wilderness area

IN THE KIAMICHI-OUACHITA Mountains of southeastern Oklahoma lies the McCurtain County Wilderness. Comprising 14,000 acres, it was established by the Oklahoma legislature in 1918, long before wilderness became a matter of prime concern to the American public. Administered by the Department of Wildlife Conservation, this magnificent woodland wilderness contains some of the largest trees in the entire Southwest including 150-foot short-leaf pines, gigantic oaks, black gum, sweet gum, holly, elm, willow, cypress, maple, ash, ironwood, and spicewood. Other types of woodland growth include dogwood, redbud, hawthorn, mistletoe, plum, grape, and greenbrier. Many ferns, mosses, mushrooms, and lichens are found here, too.

It's a lush area spiced by 52 inches of rainfall annually. Wildlife includes white-tailed deer, elk, quail, wild turkey, oppossum, rabbits, bobcat, raccoons, bald eagle, osprey, and numerous types of songbirds. Also here are pileated and red cockaded woodpeckers.

(Photo by Dean C. Graham)
Scene in the McCurtain County Wilderness, Oklahoma

Linson Creek has some of the largest sunfish in the state as well as largemouth bass.

The only human influences noted in the region are fences around the perimeter and men who periodically clear trails for fire protection. Unlike many wilderness areas, wild fires are not allowed to burn themselves out here.

This particular wilderness is used as a living yardstick by the State of Oklahoma to measure natural undisturbed processes of ecological succession or change. The quality of this environment can be used as an index standard for many parts of the state and other states in future restoration and reclamation, and it therefore becomes a wilderness workshop.

The headwaters of Broken Bow Reservoir sprawl through the center of the western section of the wilderness and permit boat and canoe traffic as well as fishing. It's an excellent means of exploring the shorelines while bird watching or photographing wildlife.

To reach the area: From the town of Broken Arrow, take SR 259 north to the Sherwood Road. Some eight miles down this road and you'll come to the lake and the boundary of the wilderness area.

WHERE TO DRIVE

Here, about all you can do in your automobile is drive into the parking lot at the area headquarters. You may see some wildlife on the way to this lot, particularly in the vicinity of the lake. While you're in the area, however, you might want to drive to the dam which impounds Broken Bow Reservoir or spend some time at Beaver's Bend State Park near the dam on the southern end of the lake. SR 259A leads to the dam site.

WHERE TO HIKE

All visitors must first check into the headquarters before entering the area. There you'll be given a set of regulations and any special recommendations. Interested individuals are allowed to make short excursions through the wilderness. Also small parties of 12 or less need only meet at the west-side boat landing at specified times on Friday, Saturday, Sunday or Monday for a two-

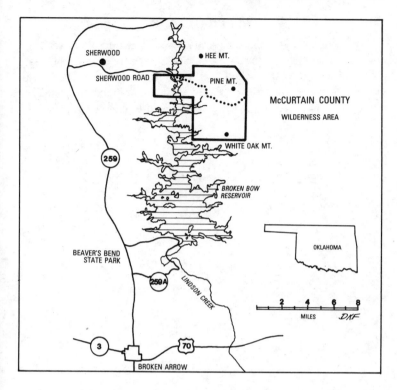

hour guided tour into the wilderness area. Larger groups must make special reservations in advance.

Hikers wishing to travel across the narrow channel of Broken Bow Lake must do so under the direction of a wilderness guide. Regulations are stringent in this wilderness and violators are dealt with harshly.

BACKPACKING OPPORTUNITIES

Backpacking is permitted, although no overnight camping is allowed. Since this is an area where rattlesnakes, copperheads, and cottonmouths make their home, it's wise to take a first-aid and snakebite kit on the trail with you.

WHERE TO CAMP

Although no camping is permitted in the wilderness area, you may camp at nearby Beaver Bend State Park, or a few miles farther to the southwest, in the Ouachita National Forest. Check with personnel in the wilderness area for their recommendations and for additional literature and maps directing you to campgrounds.

Where to Obtain Information

Public Relations
Dept. of Wildlife Conservation
P.O. Box 53465, 1801 N. Lincoln
Oklahoma City, OK 73105

wichita mountains wildlife refuge

IN SOUTHWESTERN OKLAHOMA is the 5,000-acre Charon's Gardens Wilderness and 3,900-acres North Mountain Wilderness, a part of the Wichita Mountains (National) Wildlife Refuge. Wild, rugged and weathered, the area stands as a symbol of the Old West on the threshold of modern times.

When this area of Oklahoma was opened for homesteading in 1901, a sizable portion of the heart of the Wichita Mountains was preserved and in 1905, President Teddy Roosevelt, by executive order, established a wildlife refuge here. Originally, it was established to protect all species of wildlife, but since 1905 it has been an area primarily concerned with the preservation of the American bison, Texas long-horn cattle and elk. In fact, this is considered America's most authentic herd of Texas long-horn cattle. Some 300 longhorns are now roaming the range here as well as some 600 buffalo and 500 elk. Other wildlife includes white-tailed deer, raccoon, beaver, armadillos, coyotes, fox, prairie dogs,

179

(U.S. Fish and Wildlife Service Photo by E.P. Haddon)
Longhorn steers at the Wichita Mountains Wildlife Refuge, Oklahoma

and other small animals. Quail, wild turkey and Oklahoma's state bird—the scissor-tailed flycatcher—are also found here.

The refuge's 20 or so lakes provide habitat for migratory waterfowl during spring and autumn flights. Both bald and golden eagles winter among the refuge's craggy peaks. Crayfish, mussels, and many species of frogs are found in the lake areas. This area has been described as an island oasis rising out of a vast prairie sea—the Great Plains. Woodlands here are largely made up of post oak and blackjack oak.

The reach the Refuge: From Cache, take 115 north and turn west on the scenic highway to Quannah Parker Visitor Center where displays can be seen and information may be obtained. If the visitor center is closed, continue on west to Refuge Headquarters.

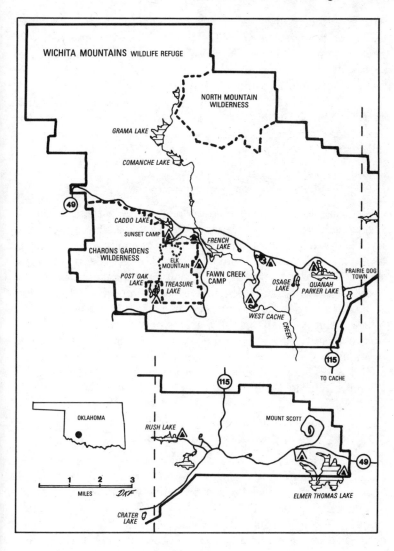

WHERE TO DRIVE

The scenic highway leading through the refuge and past the northern boundary of Charon's Gardens Wilderness provides one with an excellent driving experience. A short dead-end road leads to Sunset recreation area on the edge of the wilderness and you might also want to explore some other roads in the area leading to such spots as Treasure and Post Oaks Lakes, Caddo Lake, Fawn Creek Recreation area, French Lake or Osage Lake. Many of the lakes offer some good fishing for largemouth bass, catfish, and sunfish. The scenic highway passes a prairie dog town, Crater Lake, and provides some outstanding scenery. A spiraling three-mile drive offers a panoramic view from 2,467-foot Mt. Scott.

WHERE TO HIKE

No trails lead into the North Mountain Wilderness, which is rugged and challenging. This area is designated a Natural Research Area and is not open to public use. From the refuge headquarters, two unmarked trails lead into Charon's Garden Wilderness, one a short trail up Elk Mountain, the second bisecting the entire area to Post Oak Lake. Since rattlers are also a part of the wildlife of this area, make sure to carry a first-aid and snakebite kit with you, as well as compass, map, and an ample supply of water. You're also free to choose your own path into this wilderness if you so desire. A hiking trail five miles long is trailheaded south of French Lake and a 1⅓ mile self-guided interpretive trail, Window-on-the-Wichitas, is located at French Lake.

BACKPACKING OPPORTUNITIES

This is excellent backpacking country, although temperatures during the summer may range up to more than 100 degrees and below zero in the winter. Prepare accordingly. Since water is scarce in much of the area, it's wise to plan provisions for your water supply before going into the area. Camping is permitted only in designated recreation areas. Fires may be built only in refuge fire grates located in the recreation areas.

WHERE TO CAMP

Camping is not allowed in the wilderness areas, but several recreation areas are available to campers. Facilities include tables, fire grates, trash barrels, hand-pump water wells and restrooms. A total of seven camps and three picnic areas are provided on the refuge and there also are designated swimming beaches, intermittent streams, and canyons. Beware of buffalo and long-horn cattle; they can be dangerous.

Where to Obtain Information

Refuge Manger
Wichita Mountains Wildlife Refuge
P.O. Box 448
Cache, OK 73527

ALABAMA

sipsey river wilderness

AT THIS WRITING the Sipsey River Wilderness has merely been proposed and may indeed not become a reality. But because it is located (with the exception of 80 acres privately owned) within the Bankhead National Forest and already is open to the public, it is being included as a place offering a wilderness type experience. The wilderness includes 9,360 acres in Alabama's rugged hill country with unique topographic features.

Located at the junction of the Appalachian Plateau and the Gulf Coastal Plain, the area is a composite of features from each. Generally it is characterized by narrow ridges and deep U-shaped drainages including the canyons of Sipsey Fork and and its tributaries of the Black Warrior River. Already designated a natural area is Bee Branch.

The wilderness provides a great diversity of plant and wildlife unequalled in all of Alabama. The ridgetops produce certain types of vegetation distinctly different from the side slopes and the alluvial

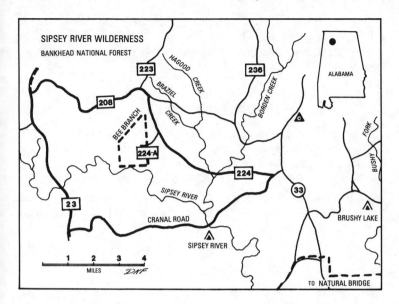

plain of the river. Mountain laurel, silverbell and viburnum grow profusely here. A total of 55 species of fish including whopper large-mouth bass, 53 kinds of animals and 18 species of reptiles and amphibians are found here. Wild turkey and white-tailed deer abound.

Climate is warm and wet, mild in winter and hot in summer with temperatures often exceeding 90 degrees. Annual precipitation is 52 inches and flash floods are common along the Sipsey, causing it to be a potential hazard to hikers in the canyons area. Beware.

To reach the area: SR 33 off US 278 at Natural Bridge leads directly past east boundary of the area, then take Forest Service Road 224 and 224-A to Bee Branch Scenic Area, which is center of wilderness area.

WHERE TO DRIVE

Several Forest Service roads bound the wilderness area and provide the motorist good insight into its geography. These include Cranal Road along the southern boundary, FS Road 208 along the northern portions. FS Road 224 and 224-A leading to the Bee

Branch Scenic Area provide excellent opportunity to view the area, although these may later be closed to motor traffic and open only to hikers and backpackers. Other roads you might like to explore include FS 223 and 236.

WHERE TO HIKE

No established hiking trails lead into the area presently, although some old roadbeds left by vacated homesteads before the turn of the century may be followed by those wishing to hike. Also, late fall to early spring, one may explore the woodland at his leisure, making his own trail, being particularly cautious around the rims and steep slopes of the canyons as well as flash floods along the streams.

BACKPACKING OPPORTUNITIES

Backpacking is discouraged, but not prohibited in the area. No facilities available and stream water for drinking is not recommended without treatment. Positively bring out all litter and do not—do not—camp along river flood plain.

WHERE TO CAMP

Campgrounds are located along Sipsey River off Cranal Road and at Brushy Lake just east of the area. At both spots are scenic nature trails which wind below high rock bluffs. No modern facilities at either.

Where to Obtain Information

Black Warrior Ranger Station
U.S. Forest Service
Haleyville, AL 35565

MISSISSIPPI

gulf islands
national seashore

ALONG THE FLORIDA and Mississippi Gulf coasts are a number of islands which were established in 1971 as a National Seashore under the administration of the National Park Service. All parts of Gulf Islands won't provide one with a wilderness experience, of course. In fact, none of those in Florida waters should be considered, but two of those in Mississippi waters—Petit Bois and Horn—as well as a portion of Ship Island do indeed represent the qualities found in wilderness. The entire National Seashore ultimately will include 125,000 acres.

The islands provide some excellent saltwater fishing territory and, of course, no license is required. Since the climate is traditionally warm and humid, the islands can generally be visited year-around. Forests on the islands consist mostly of slash pine groves, being stunted by periodic violent ocean storms. The dunes are held in place largely by sea oats, pennyworts and salt grass.

Located in Mississippi Sound, the islands are an important habi-

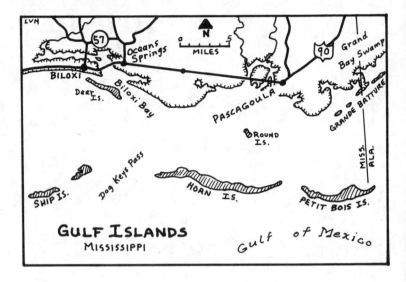

GULF ISLANDS
MISSISSIPPI

tat for tern, common egret, great blue heron and other waterfowl. During winter, the islands become a haven for blue and snow geese, many species of ducks and water birds. Seldom will one find greater solitude than on Horn or Petit Bois islands.

To reach the area: Excursion boats from May to Labor Day sail out of Gulfport and Biloxi to Ship Island. Spring and fall schedules vary. Visits to Petit Bois and Horn are by private boat or you may charter a boat from Biloxi or Gulfport to take you there.

WHERE TO DRIVE

The only part of the National Seashore you can drive to is Davis Bayou at Ocean Springs, Miss., where are located a campground and picnic area. But that won't offer you any type of wilderness experience. On a clear day the islands can be seen occasionally from shore, but at such great distance little can be derived from observing them. Consequently, this wilderness experience is not for the motorist.

WHERE TO HIKE

No trails have been established on either of the islands, but you may choose your own. Except for slash pine thickets, marshes, tidal pools, and ponds, much of the area remains open enough to hike over. And the islands are not large enough that becoming lost is a danger. Carry your own water. And also a first-aid pack and snakebite kit. Insect repellent and protection from sunburn are necessary in summer. There are cottonmouth moccasins and copperheads on the islands. Shelling is permitted.

BACKPACKING OPPORTUNITIES

Backpackers are welcome on the islands. And this activity provides an excellent means for getting away from the crowds. Neither of the islands—aside from the portion of Ship Island where Fort Massachusetts is located—are ever crowded.

WHERE TO CAMP

Primitive camping is permitted on the eastern portion of Ship Island, western tips of Horn and Petit Bois, in the Chimney Area of Horn Island, near the Ranger Station, on the eastern tips of both islands and along the inside beach near the trees on Petit Bois. Consult a park ranger for more explicit locations. Driftwood may be used for firewood. Drinking water is available at the Ranger Station on Horn Island and at the Chimney Area. And, of course, an established campground is operated at Davis Bayou.

Where to Obtain Information

Park Manager
Gulf Islands Nat'l Seashore
P.O. Box T
Ocean Springs, MS 39564

LOUISIANA

atchafalaya swamp

THE ATCHAFALAYA BASIN is a vast wild place in southern Louisiana where Boy Scouts sojourn for adventure. It's both a river and a swamp, a basin for the overflowing floodwaters of the Mississippi that provides mile upon mile of canoe water for a unique wilderness experience. While it also is a navigable waterway for larger boats and while civilization is never far away, including occasional reminders of man's inroads, there are here nonetheless some 830,000 acres of primitive territory as wild as any parcel of real estate in America.

The area is largely coastal marshland that extends south of the Bayou Teche natural levee to the Gulf of Mexico. Although much of the land mass in the Atchafalaya is privately owned, the waterways are open. Many can only be navigated by canoe or johnboat. Piroques, the Cajun canoe, are popular. But the State of Louisiana has established public domain over 23,000 acres as a recreation area near I-10 in the Grand Lake region of the Basin.

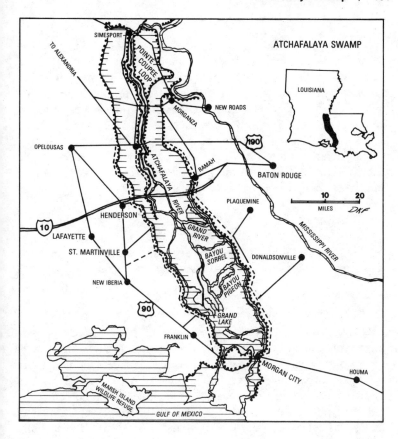

The Swamp produces excellent largemouth bass, bream, and crappie fishing, as well as whopper catfish. During winter, substantial colonies of Canada and snow geese and other waterfowl congregate here. Other inhabitants include squirrels, deer, alligators, otter, panther, and bobcat.

In late winter and spring, the Atchafalaya often is in flood and dangerous to boat or canoe. Summers are often too hot with temperatures ranging in the mid to high 90s. Autumn and early winter is the most ideal time to sample Atchafalaya.

To reach the Swamp: Take I-10 west of Baton Rouge to SR I south. You'll find numerous launching places along the levee.

WHERE TO DRIVE

Although minimum speeds are in effect, one of the best ways to really see the Atchafalaya from automobile is via I-10. It gives one an elevated bird's-eye view of miles of prime wild territory studded with cypress. You'll also see from this highway multitudes of birds and other wildlife. Other great roads to drive in the area include SR 75 west of Seymourville, SR 70 to Morgan City, and SR 96 along the west side of the swamp. The Henderson area is particularly interesting for motorists. On either side of the Atchafalaya are roads (gravel) atop the levees which permit you to study the swamp from your automobile at closer range.

WHERE TO HIKE

There are no hiking trails in the area, although you can hike the levee roads, which have very little automotive traffic.

CANOE TRAILS

No canoe trails have been established, but with topographic maps you can go virtually anywhere in the swamp. Many high spots exist where one may pitch camp. Jungle hammocks are desirable for camping here, too, which allow one to get off the ground, since cottonmouth moccasins are plentiful in the swamp.

Canoe rentals are available both in New Orleans and Lafayette as well as cartop carriers, paddles, and life jackets. If you desire guide service or would like to join a group tour of the Atchafalaya, contact the Baton Rouge Sierra Club, Box 624, Baton Rouge, 70821.

BACKPACKING OPPORTUNITIES

Although no hiking trails are established, one may backpack the levees and pitch camp alongsiae the Atchafalaya virtually any place along its 140-mile length.

WHERE TO CAMP

No organized campgrounds. Pitch your tent in the swamp at any place not posted with "No Trespassing" signs. Several campgrounds are located within short driving distance of the swamp, however, including Lafayette, Pierre Park, and St. Martinville.

Where to Obtain Information

Atchafalaya Basin Division
Dept. of Public Works
State Capitol Bldg.
Box 44361
Baton Rouge, LA 70804

Baton Rouge Sierra Club
P.O. Box 624
Baton Rouge, LA 70821

Tourist Development Comm.
Box 44291 Capitol Station
Baton Rouge, LA 70804

kisatchie hills wilderness

THE KISATCHIE HILLS, located in the Kisatchie Ranger District of the Kisatchie National Forest, includes some 10,000 acres of land—some exceptionally rugged terrain for this part of central Louisiana. Here are found several mesas, buttes and sandstone outcroppings amid a natural background of Longleaf pine. The entire area is a botanical garden with more than 150 varieties of woody plants and vines. Flowering begins in late winter and reaches its peak in April with dogwood, wild azalea, redbud and yuka being the more common species. The colors during this blooming season are fantastic.

The Kisatchie Hills is a bird watcher's paradise with more than 250 species. More common ones include the pileated woodpecker, cardinal, pine warbler, brownheaded nuthatch; two rare species here are the red cockaded woodpecker and the Bachman sparrow. Occasionally a bald eagle is spotted, for they migrate to this area during the winter months. The Kisatchie Hills has long

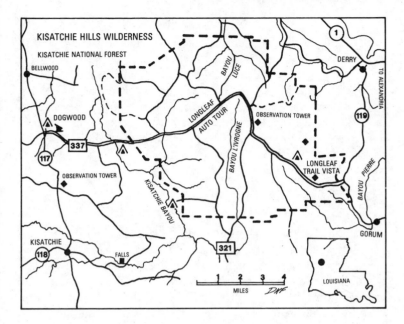

been managed as a scenic area by the US Forest Service, but it provides a unique wilderness type experience.

To reach the area: From Alexandria, take SR 1 northwest to SR 119 south at Derry. This leads to the Kisatchie Hills area.

WHERE TO DRIVE

SR 119 leads into the Kisatchie Hills, but the Forest Service has established a self-guided auto tour of the area which gives one considerable opportunity to sample it. Called the Longleaf Auto Tour, it offers an encounter with many interesting features, is about 25 miles long, and may require anywhere from an hour to a day, depending upon how much time you'd like to spend stopping or exploring the nearby woodland. Various points of interest have been labeled to include some of the legend, history, nature, and geology of the area. A brochure about the tour is available from the forest headquarters or ranger station.

WHERE TO HIKE

No hiking trails have been established in the section referred to as wilderness, although one may hike the same 25-mile road used by the auto tour if he desires. Traffic is normally light, particularly during the week when one may have little concern for automotive travel. If you desire to enter the area, the woodland, particularly in fall and winter, is not so dense that one cannot choose his own trail into some of the more remote sections. Some small streams and bayous bisect portions of the area, but the water is not usable without boiling or chemical treatment.

BACKPACKING OPPORTUNITIES

One may backpack anywhere within the area, choosing his own primitive campsite. Beware of poisonous snakes including cottonmouth, rattlers, and copperheads. Be sure to take a first-aid and snakebite kit. Most of the bayous and streams are located along the extreme northern and southern portions of the area. Also carry a good insect repellent during the warm months for mosquitoes are a problem.

WHERE TO CAMP

Choose your own primitive campsites at any place in the Kisatchie Hills. Best sites, of course, are along the bayous where you'll have access to water. An established campground— Longleaf Trail Vista—with three campsites is located along the perimenter of the area and includes a picnic shelter, drinking water, scenic area, and short nature trails.

Where to Obtain Information

District Ranger
U.S. Forest Service
Natchitoches, LA 71457

Forest Supervisor
Kitsatchie Nat'l Forest
2500 Shreveport Hwy.
Pineville, LA 71360

saline bayou wilderness

SALINE BAYOU, LOCATED in Winn Parish on the Winn Ranger District of the Kisatchie National Forest, includes some 5,000 acres of land in a corridor along an eight-mile section of Saline Bayou, a state-designated scenic river. Although this area was lumbered long ago before acquisition by the US Forest Service, nature has virtually covered all signs of man's inroads

The primary wilderness attraction here are the huge cypress trees, gums, and oaks that line the stream banks. Best way to sample this bit of Louisiana wilderness, however, is not by hiking (one would need to carve his way with a machete through the dense undergrowth to do that), but by canoe or small rowboat or raft. The current is very slow in this bayou, but there are alligators, numerous turtles and a multitude of birds in the area. There are some places where one can debark and sit under a giant cypress to listen to the sounds of the swamp. The Saline moves its coffee-colored waters through habitat varying from red clay to deep sandhill country to upland swamps.

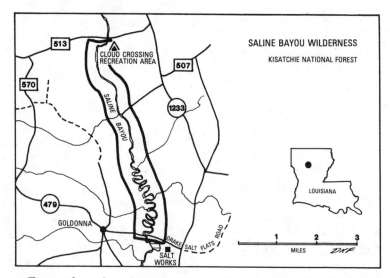

Except for a few short stretches and bends, the bayou is narrow enough over its entire length to be bridged by a fallen tree. Such trees generally present the major obstacles to float trips.

Best time to enjoy the bayou is from December through mid-July. During late summer and fall, its waters are so shallow that travel becomes difficult.

Red and gray squirrels, fox, raccoons, white-tailed deer, and bobcat roam the swamp areas along the bayou. Cottonmouth, rattlers, and copperhead snakes along with numerous harmless varieties are located here. Take along an insect repellent, particularly in May through July; the mosquitoes are vicious.

To reach the Bayou: From Goldonna, take SR 479 northwest to Forest Service Road 570 north to FS Road 513 east. This leads to the Cloud Crossing Recreation Area which is a good point to begin your float trip down the Saline. At high-water-level times of the year, you may float portions of the bayou north of here, particularly in a shallow draft canoe or piroque. But your best bet is to launch at the recreation area and float south.

WHERE TO DRIVE

No roads border the Saline Wilderness, but you can see a portion of it from the Cloud Crossing Recreation Area on the north or from the Drake Salt Flats Road on the southern end. Another road—Forest Service Road 507—leads to the banks of the bayou, giving the motorist an opportunity to watch float trips in progress or to pick up canoeists or launch them if they want to shorten their trip.

WHERE TO HIKE

There are a few places where one may hike for very short distances along the bayou, but generally this is not suitable hiking terrain because of the heavy undergrowth.

BACKPACKING OPPORTUNITIES

Backpacking is permitted, but since there are no trails, the terrain discourages it.

WHERE TO CANOE

If you wish to take a short trip to see if you like the bayou, try floating some two miles to the "panther hole." Here a good dirt access road reaches the bayou and makes a good take-out point. Be careful not to miss it, for another seven miles of dark water is ahead before you reach the next take-out point.

From Cloud Crossing to the Salt Works is about 10 miles or six hours of easy floating. The last couple of miles consist of constant switchbacks. Two canoes can be traveling downstream in opposite directions within 10 feet of one another.

The Salt Works area is a large open flat with ample room for parking several cars. Thefts often occur, however, when cars are left overnight. Best time to float here is during winter or early spring. Weather is usually mild during that time, there's ample water level and no insects or snakes.

WHERE TO CAMP

Cloud Crossing Recreation Area offers 13 campsites, drinking water, fishing, and primitive toilets. There are also numerous primitive sites along the bayou where one may set up a canoe camp. Be doubly sure you police up the area before you leave (in fact, leave it cleaner than you found it).

Where to Obtain Information

District Ranger
U.S. Forest Service
Winnfield, LA 71483

Forest Supervisor
Kisatchie Nat'l Forest
2500 Shreveport Hwy
Pineville, LA 71360

TEXAS

aransas national wildlife refuge

NATURALIST ROBERT ALLEN once wrote: "The sight of a whooping crane in the air is an experience packed with beauty and drama ... In grim aspect of the features, in the whole trim of the birds as they move, silently now, there is a dignity and sense of un-conquered wildness, of an obstinate will to survive. We watch them with admiration and with hope. In spite of its glowing reality, it is like a brief and unexpected look at the world as it was in the begin-ning."

It is because of this—the whooping crane—that I have included Aransas in this book, for therein lies a sense of wildness for each who looks upon these magnificent birds. And Aransas is the place to find them. This 54,829-acre refuge occupies Blackjack Peninsula along the Gulf Coast of Texas. Made up chiefly of grasslands, live oak and redbay thickets, stands of blackjack oak and tidal marshes, the deep sandy soils of the Blackjack Peninsula make ideal habitat for the nearly extinct whooping cranes. Besides

201

Whooping cranes in flight at the Aransas National Wildlife Refuge

the cranes it is also home for spoonbills, wild turkey, white-tailed deer, javalinas, alligators, armadillos, and many smaller animals and birds. Herons, pelicans, curlews, and thousands of ducks and

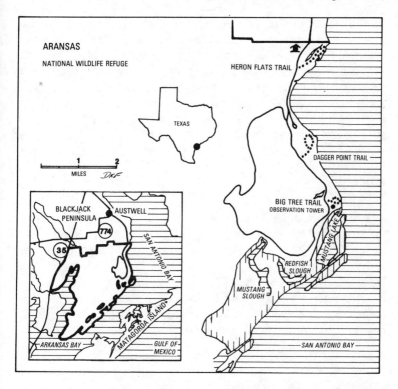

geese come here to feed and rest on the mud flats along the tidal marshes. One of the picnic areas in a motte of oak trees serves as a roost for turkey vultures at night.

At few spots in America will one find a greater array of wildlife than at Aransas National Wildlife Refuge. Because of this gathering of nature's children, the wildlife refuge certainly can provide one with at least a semi-wilderness, if not a wilderness experience.

To reach the Refuge: From Corpus Christi, take SR 35 east to FR road 2040 through Austwell. The refuge headquarters is seven miles SE of Austwell.

WHERE TO DRIVE

SR 35 borders one side of the refuge and you may, in fact, see some wildlife from this highway. On the refuge (and you must register daily before touring there) some 20 miles of road wind through meadows, thickets, and marshes as well as along the shore and tidal flats. The refuge is open sunrise to sunset daily.

From your atuomobile, you may see some of the larger animals—deer, javelinas (or peccary), alligators, plus such smaller species as armadillos, raccoons, and snakes. The most rewarding time to visit here is from November through March when migratory waterfowl and the whooping cranes are present.

WHERE TO HIKE

Traffic is slow and usually light on weekdays, so one can hike the 20-mile loop drive through the refuge and be much more likely to see wildlife. Three short nature spur trails lead off this main drive—Heron Flats Trail, Dagger Point, and Big Tree Trail. The latter was named after the point where Jean Lafitte is reputed to have disbanded his crew and buried enough treasure to ransom a nation. The Big Tree stand he referred to can be reached by trail near the observation tower and is a favorite bird watching spot.

BACKPACKING OPPORTUNITIES

To avoid disturbing wildlife, no backpacking is permitted.

WHERE TO CAMP

No camping is permitted on the refuge, but there are established campgrounds within a short driving distance. Check with the refuge headquarters for information on this or with the Texas Tourism Comm. in Austin.

Where to Obtain Information

Refuge Manager
Aransas Nat'l Wildlife Refuge
P.O. Box 68
Austwell, TX 77950

Director
Texas Tourist Comm.
Capitol Station
Austin, TX 78763

big bend national park

ALONG THE GREAT curve made by the Rio Grande between the border of west Texas and Mexico lies a great wilderness—Big Bend National Park. While not a designated wilderness, Big Bend is a vast and unique place, 708,000 acres of desert and mountains, streams, canyons, and arroyos that more resemble Mexico than the U.S. Here you can see well-preserved remains of animals that roamed the earth millions of years ago, smell the aroma of creosote bushes, listen to the early morning yowl of coyotes, and the bristling squeal of the javelina. Four species of rattlesnakes and copperhead live here, all poisonous. There are also numerous scorpions and tarantulas. Beware, too, of the cactus. These plants and many of the other trees and shrubs are well armed with spines that inflict painful injury.

A major wilderness experience may be had by raft or canoe floating sections of the Rio Grande River through Santa Elena and Mariscal canyons. The high sheer walls seem to overhang the winding river. Boquillas Canyon, cut through the Sierra del Carmen

(Photo by W. Ray Scott)

Afloat in the Santa Elena Canyon, Big Bend National Park, Texas. Rock walls rise more than 1600 feet separating Mexico (left) from the U.S.A. (right).

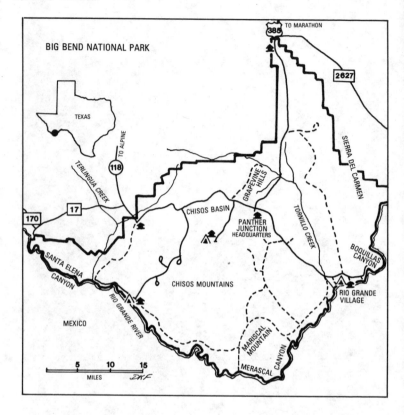

by the Rio Grande, is 25 miles in length, the longest of Big Bend's famous gorges. In the evening the sun seems to set fire to the face of the Sierra del Carmen.

Horses can be rented in the park. Year-around temperatures make this park accessible anytime, but summer heat can be a problem with the thermometer ranging over 100 degrees in some desert areas. Flash floods are a problem and sometimes come without warning down dry desert streams. Beware.

To reach the Park: From Marathon, take US 385 south to the entrance; from Alpine, take SR 118.

WHERE TO DRIVE

Roads in the park are open to the motorist. Many miles of back-country dirt roads lead to points of interest and spots worth exploring. One can have some fascinating experiences by auto in Big Bend, including the drive from the Basin to Santa Elena Canyon on the Rio Grande, or a second drive to Rio Grande Village and Boquillas Canyon. Normally, each drive would take less than an hour, but because most motorists want to stop for picture-taking or viewing the scenery, it may take several hours to make the round trip. Consult with experts at the Park Headquarters at Panther Junction or the Information Booth at the Basin for their recommendations on other motoring trips.

WHERE TO HIKE

More than 30 trails of varying lengths (from 1 to 33 miles) and challenges are located here. A booklet called *Hiker's Guide to the Developed Trails and Primitive Routes* is available from the National Park Service. It gives detailed breakdowns on each of the trails and what you may encounter along them. A second guidebook—*Guide to the Backcountry Roads and the River*—is also offered. Many of these back-country roads are excellent for hiking and will provide a wilderness-type experience. Make sure to carry an ample supply of water while hiking here, as well as comforts in case of becoming over-heated or incurring sunburn. Be sure to carry a first-aid kit since no doctors or nurses are available in the park.

BACKPACKING OPPORTUNITIES

Virtually all the trails in Big Bend are suitable for backpacking but campsites are restrictive. Just make sure to get a back-country permit from a Park Ranger and not to leave any signs of your visit. Consult the hiker's guide booklet before planning your backpack trip.

WHERE TO CAMP

Primitive camping is permitted along some trails. Since the ecology in this arid country is indeed fragile, be sure to check with the Park Ranger before going on the trail. Water availability again is a problem, so also check with the ranger on this. Make doubly sure you're well away from dry stream beds before pitching camp, lest you awaken facing a wall of water from a flash flood upstream. Lightning also can be a problem here. Three established campgrounds are located in the park.

Where to Obtain Information

Superintendent
Big Bend Nat'l Park, TX 79834

big slough wilderness

IN THE NORTHERN reaches of the Davy Crockett National Forest, the Big Slough comprises some 1,500 acres of swamp and heavy forests made up mostly of bottomland hardwoods such as sweet gum and water oak. It's an ideal canoe area with some hiking possibilities. Temperatures are muggy hot and uncomfortable May to September, mild in winter. The Neches River and adjoining sloughs are narrow, winding, shallow, and ideal for canoe trails. No white water. Good fishing for largemouth bass, bream and catfish.

Wildlife includes cottonmouth snakes, rattlers, copperheads, coral snakes (all poisonous), alligators, pileated woodpecker, great blue heron, white-tailed deer, fox, raccoon, and opposum. The Neches River lowlands and the adjoining Big Slough provide an unexpected encounter for those interested in botany.

To reach the area: From Lufkin take SR 103 to Ratcliff, and turn north. The canoe launching area is located six miles from Ratcliff at Scurlock's Camp, just east of FS road 517-A.

211

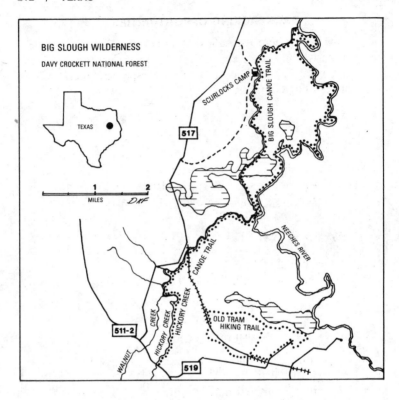

BIG SLOUGH WILDERNESS

DAVY CROCKETT NATIONAL FOREST

TEXAS

MILES

SCURLOCKS CAMP

517

BIG SLOUGH CANOE TRAIL

NECHES RIVER

CANOE TRAIL

HICKORY CREEK

HICKORY CREEK

WALNUT CREEK

511-2

OLD TRAM HIKING TRAIL

519

WHERE TO DRIVE

All of FS Road 517 is on the national forest, giving one a good look at some of the representative plantlife.

WHERE TO HIKE

The Old Tram Hiking Trail extends in a grand loop through the southern portion of the Big Slough area, providing approximately three miles of educational adventure for the hiker. This trail also connects up with another portion of the Slough over Hickory Creek to FS Road 511 C.

BACKPACKING OPPORTUNITIES

Since the policy here is to allow camping anywhere on national forest property, this area presents good backpacking opportunities. The main challenge is finding a suitable spot to pitch a tent. Beware of poisonous snakes.

WHERE TO CANOE

Two excellent canoe trails exist in the area, one a loop trail extending some seven miles allowing one to return to the launch location. The slow pace of the current here allows opportunity for bird watching, picture-taking, and enjoying the scenery. Greater solitude cannot be found in all of Texas than on the Big Slough canoe trail. The other trail extends for three miles on Hickory Creek, from FS Road 511 to Big Slough Canoe Trail. By using both trails, one can travel a total of 13 miles.

Caution: The canoe trails cannot be traveled during extended dry periods.

WHERE TO CAMP

Choose your own spot and pitch camp. Several good spots along Hickory Creek are available. Also camping is available near the town of Ratcliff only approximately 6 miles away in an established Forest Service campground.

Where to Obtain Information

Neches District Ranger
U.S. Forest Sercice
East Loop 304
Crockett, TX 75835

Forest Supervisor
U.S. Forest Service
P.O. Box 969
Lufkin, TX 75901

big thicket

IN SOUTHEAST TEXAS is a remarkable wilderness most appropriately named the Big Thicket. It is literally that in every respect and although it is today broken into spotty remnants, you have no difficulty in identifying it. For once you have reached the Big Thicket, the dense woodland suddenly becomes a curtain dropped at the edge of the roadway. Beyond it you can see nothing but the darkened chambers of the most dense vegetation found anywhere in North America. Yet the boundaries of the Big Thicket are disputable; no one—even those who have spent all their lives there—can agree on just where the Thicket begins or ends.

Initially the area known to the Alabama-Coushatta Indians (whose reservation still lies on the northern edge) as the Big Woods embraced some 3-million acres. But generally now, the area is considered to lie principally in five counties—Hardin, Polk, Liberty, Tyler, and Jasper.

A study done in 1965 by the National Park Service in preparation

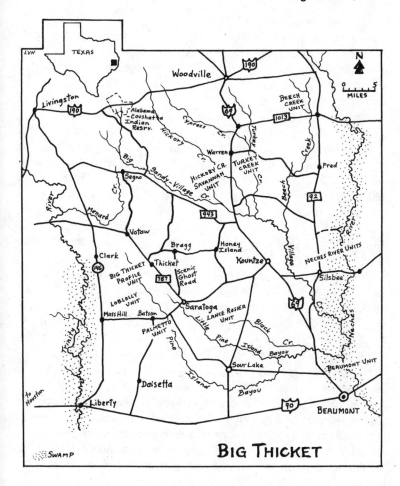

BIG THICKET

for making it into a national park considers that part worthy of public domain—a veritable wilderness to be preserved for posterity. In late 1974 Congress enacted a bill creating the Big Thicket National Park. Very little of the Thicket (in 1974) is on public land. Most of it is owned by lumber companies who really don't mind if visitors hike the old logging roads and trails as long as they don't litter or molest the forest. A total of 87,000 acres eventually will make up the national park.

Vegetation consists of palmetto, live oaks, virgin beech, magnolia, sassafras, dogwood, wild grapevines, and giant loblolly pines. The Big Thicket is a place into which Mother Nature tossed a little bit of everything—a melting pot of plants and animals indigenous to the east and west, north and south, the temperate and sub-tropic zones.

One may find here, for instance, up to nine species of insect-eating plants including sundew, bladderwort, butterwort, and pitcher plants. Every poisonous snake found in the U.S. is found in the Big Thicket—coral, rattlesnake, cottonmouth, and copperhead. Also here is the nearly extinct ivory-billed woodpecker, the pileated, the bald eagle, alligator, white-tailed deer, red and gray fox, raccoon, armadillo, cottontail rabbit, and squirrel. The American white egret, road-runner, great blue heron, green heron, and numerous other birds are found here. But mainly the Big Thicket is a botanical paradise.

More than 1,000 species of fungi and algae alone are located here as well as some 40 varieties of wild orchids, 25 species and subspecies of ferns and thousands of wild flowers. Herbs range from ginseng to the more common wax myrtle. There's also scarlet buckeye, wild phlox, wild azaleas, wild iris, and trumpet vine. A giant magnolia believed to be more than 1,000-years-old, a holly tree 80-feet tall recognized as the largest of its kind in the world, and many other unusual specimens of plantlife can be found here.

The Park Service in their study includes what they call a "string of pearls"—features believed to represent a profile of the area—a virgin beech forest, bogs, a lush growth of insect-eating plants, an untouched cypress swamp, a large stand of virgin loblolly pine, and scenic stretches of the Pine Island Bayou and the Neches River.

To reach the area: From Livingston take US 190 east to the Alabama-Coushatta Indian Reservation on the northern edge of the Big Thicket; from Beaumont, take US 69 to Kountze in the midst of the Big Thicket.

WHERE TO DRIVE

From Livingston, take US 190 east to the Alabama-Coushatta Indian Reservation on the northern edge of the Big Thicket. Here you may take one of several tours into the Big Thicket and learn the Indian version of the Big Thicket story. Continue east to Woodville for a visit to the Big Thicket Gardens which give you a good concept of the varied botanical growth found here; this will help you identify plants you later see in the wilderness portions of the Thicket. Drive south on US 69 to Kountze, then west to Saratoga, home of the Big Thicket Association headquarters and museum. You'll want to visit this, for it gives you an education on the geography and wildlife of the Thicket; also available is advice on how best you can enjoy the Thicket and experience it.

FM Road 787 through Thicket and Vowaw is well worth the drive. Ask the attendant at the museum about the Ghost Road, a dirt backroad through the Big Thicket (eight miles long) which also gives one a great opportunity to explore the Thicket by automobile.

WHERE TO HIKE

In San Jacinto County is an 1130-acre tract adjacent to a roadside park just off SR 150 south of Coldspring. Numerous short trails lead from the park into the Thicket including the Big Thicket Scenic Trail, maintained by the U.S. Forest Service, where visitors may see many of the plants and trees native to the Big Thicket. The trail leads to nearby Double Lake Recreation Area which offers swimming, picnicking, and nature studies. Although it's not quite a wilderness experience, you might also like to hike the Ghost Road. Its soft dirt surface provides excellent walking and there's virtually no automotive traffic.

Numerous old logging roads lead through the area on private timber company holdings. Most of these companies don't object to hikers using the roads as long as they leave no litter and in no way abuse the forest. But keep off land that's posted "No Trespassing." The Association also maintains a nature trail in Rosier Park at the edge of Saratoga.

BACKPACKING OPPORTUNITIES

Best opportunities for backpacking include the old logging roads or the parts included in the National Forest near Double Lake

Recreation Area at Coldspring off SR 150. Make sure to gain permission before backpacking on private property. Although water is plentiful in most parts of the Thicket, it's not suitable for drinking and must be boiled or chemically treated. Beware of snakes and make sure to carry first-aid and snakebite kits. Also carry some drinking water.

The surface of much of the Thicket is a damp, soggy woods, although there are some high and dry areas, depending on the season. Spring and early summer months constitute the rainiest season, although the area has considerable rain in winter as well. Winter is considered by many the best time to backpack in the area.

WHERE TO CAMP

The Trinity and Neches rivers, generally considered to form the western and eastern boundaries of the Big Thicket, are both excellent canoe streams with many sandbars where one may camp. The current is an easy one, making the streams adaptable to even novice canoeists. Pine Island Bayou also is an excellent area from which to experience the Big Thicket. One may launch near Sour Lake and float to the Neches River. Village Creek is an especially good stream for novices and offers outstanding scenic values.

WHERE TO CAMP

Although one may do primitive camping with permission of some of the private timberland holdings along old logging roads, other camping places are few. In the Sam Houston National Forest at Double Lake Recreation Area is an established campground and there's also one at the Alabama-Coushatta Indian Reservation. Some private campgrounds are located in the area. Consult The Big Thicket Association for locations and recommendations.

Where to Obtain Information

Big Thicket Association
Saratoga, TX 77585

Public Information Officer
National Park Service
Southwest Region
Box 728
Santa Fe, NM 87501

Superintendent
Sam Houston Nat'l Forest
Lufkin, TX 75901

Texas Tourist Development Agency
Box 12008 Capitol Station
Austin, TX 78711

caddo lake

NO PART OF this vast natural lake astride the border of northeast Texas and western Louisiana has been officially designated or even proposed as wilderness, but the tail-water portions, all of which are located in Texas, certainly offer a wilderness-type experience. It's a shallow lake studded with dense forest of cypress.

Through these are boat or canoe trails where one may lose himself from civilization for days on end. Just enough high ground exists to pitch camp. There are cottonmouth moccasins, alligators, a wide array of birds to include the great blue heron, common egret, golden eagle, osprey, red-tailed hawk and great barred owl, bobcat, white-tailed deer and numerous smaller animals that make this home.

The lake provides some of the best crappie and bream fishing in the South, yet one dare not go into the cypress forest unless he has a map and compass and knows how to read them well or has a native guide to bring him safely back to his starting point. In some

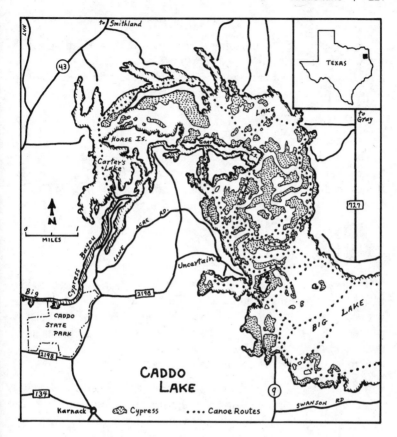

CADDO
LAKE

Karnack 〇 🌿 Cypress • • • • Canoe Routes

places, the great bald cypress is so dense and so draped with
Spanish moss that sunlight seldom penetrates, yet one can work a
canoe into these areas and enjoy the solitude of this place as
though civilization did not exist. Several movies have been made in
the area because of its pristine qualities.

To reach the area: From Marshall, Texas, take SR 43 to Farm-
Ranch Road 2198 which leads to the village of Uncertain. This is a
good place to launch a canoe for your trip to explore Caddo Lake.

WHERE TO DRIVE

The Round-Up Road from Uncertain to the Blair Landing Road allows the motorist to view a portion of the wooded lake. SR22 and 23 also is an interesting drive as well as several roads leading south from the town of Gethsemane, on SR 49 north of the lake.

WHERE TO HIKE

No trails exist around the lake, but most of the roads are lightly traveled and you might like to hike along some of them to sample the overall atmosphere. A few short trails exist in nearby Caddo Lake State park which includes some of the same type terrain and atmosphere as Caddo Lake itself.

BACKPACKING AND CANOEING OPPORTUNITIES

There are no backpacking opportunities here, unless you consider your backpacking from a canoe. This is the best way to see the lake, which normally is calm in the upper reaches. But many islands and open channels exist here, making the lake appear as a maze, so make sure you have a good map and compass, and know how to use them before going into the area.

WHERE TO CAMP

You can choose your own campsite on one of the many islands in the lake for a primitive setting, but make sure you carry out everything you take in. Leave nothing but footprints. If you prefer an established campground, you may find some private ones along the lakeshore or a fine campground at Caddo State Park, just a short distance down the road.

Where to Obtain Information

Chamber of Commerce
Marshall, TX 75670

guadalupe mountains national park

IN THE ARID portions of Texas where the terrain becomes predominantly more west than east is Guadalupe Mountains National Park, established in 1972. With few improvements, the park remains a veritable vast wilderness, comprising 77,500 acres astride the highest mountains in Texas.

These are unusual mountains. From the distance they appear like any other mountain range, but closer examination will reveal a spectacular exposure of the Capitan Reef which geologists claim to be the most extensive fossil reef exposed complex on earth. The mountain range resembles a giant V-shaped wedge with El Capitan, a 2,000-foot sheer cliff at the center—with arms extending to the northeast and northwest into New Mexico.

Within these mountains and canyons is a unique remnant of forest plants and animals which have struggled for survival since Pleistocene times. Elevations range from 3,650 feet at the base of the western escarpment to 8,751 feet on the summit of Guadalupe Peak,

(NPS Photo by Fred Mang, Jr.)

Looking east to Guadalupe Peak, Guadalupe Mountains National Park, Texas

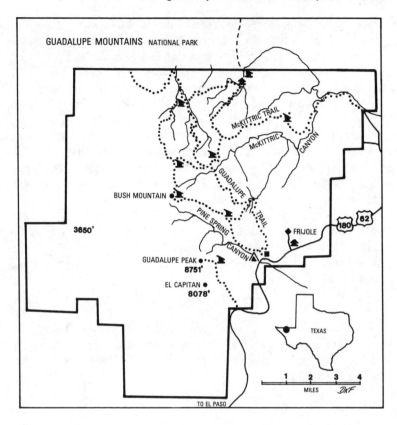

highest point in Texas. The park has diverse areas including desert lowlands, superb canyons such as McKittrick Canyon, and forested mountains. A switchback trail leads to the top of the mountains from which you can view the great Salt Basin to the west, the Delaware Basin to the south and east, and a series of deeply-cut dramatic canyons to the north.

Botanically, the area is also a mixture for here species of the Rocky Mountains reach their southern and eastern limit and mix with species from Mexico at the northern extent of their range. Plant and animals of the eastern and central plains also find their western-

most limits here. Typical of the southwestern desert are creoso-
tebush, Parry agave, lechugilla, yucca, sotol and, in the high country,
there's Douglas fir, limber pine, and aspen. In the sheltered
canyons where moisture is more abundant, ferns, big-tooth maple,
chokecherry, walnut, hophornbeam, and Texas madrone are found.

Wildlife is common including ringtail raccoon, wild turkey, mule
deer, elk, porcupine, gray fox, bobcat, black bear, and cougar. The
western diamondback and blacktailed rattlesnakes are found here; in
fact, more than 70 species of reptiles and amphibians have been
identified. Some 200 species of birds live or migrate through this
area including the golden eagle. Besides rattlesnakes, another hazard
demands your caution—climate.

Semi-arid in nature, the summers are generally warm and winters
mild. But severe and sudden changes in weather are likely to occur
with little warning. Strong winds usually occur in spring and autumn.
In summer, there may be severe electrical storms with flashflooding
in the canyons.

To reach the Park: From El Paso, take US 62 and 180 northeast
to the entrance to the park. No visitor center or park headquarters
is here, however, there is an information center at Frijole Station,
near Pine Springs.

WHERE TO DRIVE

Approximately five miles of US 62 and 180 passes through a
portion of the park just east of the mountains and a couple of spur
roads lead to the park boundary in other spots off these highways.
But in the park, few roads are open to the public. Spectacular
views of El Capitan and the eastern and western escarpments can
be seen from the U.S. highways. At Guadalupe Pass, roadside
picnic areas have been provided.

WHERE TO HIKE

A complex of 55 miles of hiking trails extend through many
parts of the park, many of them quite rugged and challenging.

Some routes are ill-defined and only experienced hikers who carry and are capable of using topo maps and compass should use some of them.

Maps may be purchased at the information station. Good boots and an adequate supply of water are essential. Be sure to carry first-aid and snakebite kits.

Some of the trails lead to the high country such as the Guadalupe Trail, and another leading along the crest of Bush Mountain. In the lowlands, the McKittrick Canyon Trail is most interesting. A short trail leads from US 62 to Guadalupe Peak.

BACKPACKING OPPORTUNITIES

Great opportunities for backpacking here, both in deserts and forests. Trails are faint and water may become a problem, particularly in the desert country. Backpackers should be thoroughly prepared for a most rugged experience and check in at the information station to obtain campsite locations and register. They must also check in upon return.

Wood fires are not permitted, so carry a small cookstove using container fuel. By studying thoroughly a topo map and comparing notes with park service personnel, you can determine your itinerary prior to venturing into backcountry and thereby gain greater enjoyment from your trip. (*Note*: Horseback trips are available into the area, too, but only horses accustomed to rugged boulder-strewn mountain trails should be used. Horses are not permitted in McKittrick Canyon.)

WHERE TO CAMP

Only a single primitive drive-in campground existed as of 1974—located in Pine Spring Canyon. Numerous designated back-country sites are available for backpackers. Pick up a map at the information center which will give you locations of these sites. The primitive campground at Pine Spring Canyon has pit toilets, tables, and trash cans. Water is available from the information center, a mile away.

Where to Obtain Information

Superintendent
Carlsbad Caverns Nat'l Park
3225 El Paso Road
Carlsbad, NM 88220

laguna atascosa wilderness

JUST TWENTY-FIVE MILES from the Mexican Border near the Gulf of Mexico is the Laguna Atascosa National Wildlife Refuge. Some 9,440 acres of this 45,000-acre refuge comprise the North Island Wilderness, a remote area consisting of mud flats and low-lying desert or semi-desert plains.

Thousands of birds and waterfowl of all species flock to the wilderness during winter; studies show there are 330 species on the refuge bird list and 83 nest here.

North Island is part of a small delta formed by the Arroyo Colorado, formerly a principal flood channel for the Rio Grande. In fact, a number of old stream channels cut by the Rio Grande cross the broad flats. Mud flats cover nearly half of North Island, but it is these that contribute heavily to the ecology and lifestyle of shore and wading birds. Birdlife includes two endangered species—the southern bald eagle and the American peregrine falcon.

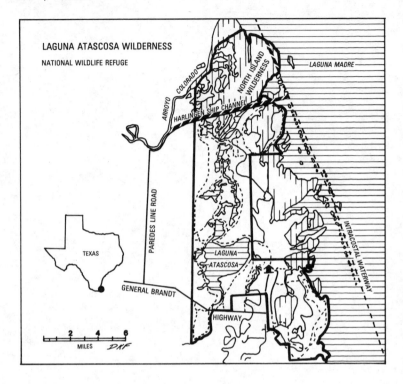

White-tailed deer and javelina may be found here as well. Among the most outstanding features of this wilderness is its pattern of coastal vegetation—a blend of semi-arid, tropical, and seashore plants. Plants like acacia, palo verde, mesquite and several species of cacti indicate semi-arid, while Texas lantana, and yaupon represent the tropical kingdom. Seashore plants such as moss flower, sea oxeye, and glasswort are also found here. The temperature is mild in winter and muggy hot in summer.

To reach the Wilderness: From Harlingen take FM Road 106 through Rio Honda to the refuge. This leads to the refuge. The trip to the North Island Wilderness must be made by either boat or canoe, via the Harlingen Ship Channel or the Intracoastal Waterway.

WHERE TO DRIVE

No roads lead to the North Island Wilderness, but there are several roads on the adjacent national wildlife refuge which can be driven for observing wildlife and seeing some related wilderness. Since certain roads are closed at various times of the year to facilitate wildlife management, check with the refuge headquarters for recommendations on where to drive once you arrive in the area.

WHERE TO HIKE

Again, certain seasons may compel the closing of the North Island unit to entry, but when it's open to the public, one may walk along the area bordering the mudflats for closeup studies of various birdlife. Best way to reach it is by canoe or small boat along the Harlingen Ship Channel or the Intracoastal Waterway, being cautious, of course, to stay out of the path of other boats. As long as you stay close to shore, there should be no problems.

BACKPACKING OPPORTUNITIES

No backpacking nor overnight camping permitted to avoid disturbing wildlife.

WHERE TO CAMP

No camping is permitted in the wilderness or on the refuge. Camping is permitted in campgrounds nearby, however. For details, check with the refuge manager.

Where to Obtain Information

Refuge Manager
Laguna Atascosa Nat'l Wildlife Refuge
P.O. Box 2683
Harlingen, TX 78550

padre island

OFF THE TEXAS Gulf Coast is America's largest national seashore, offering a most unique wilderness experience. Padre Island, extending 113 miles, is comprised of a national seashore 80 miles long through its midsection. Here on this narrow barrier island lashed by wind and sea one may enjoy the rhythmic beat of surf, the cry of a gull, the singular fragrance borne by wind off the sea, mile upon mile of firm wet beach to walk upon, dunes of dry clean sand, and an inspiring solitude.

The island's width ranges from a few hundred yards to more than three miles. It's separated from the mainland by a shallow body of water at some points ten miles wide. Between the gulf and the lagoon lies—first, the wide clean beach, which in places gives way to small shells; next, an alignment of sand dunes that sometimes pitch upward 40 feet; then grassy flats; and last, a vaguely defined shoreline that seems to merge with the water of the lagoon.

The shell beaches indicate an abundance of clams, marine snails,

White pelicans nest in teeming rookeries on Bird Island in the Intercoastal Waterway behind Padre Island, Texas.

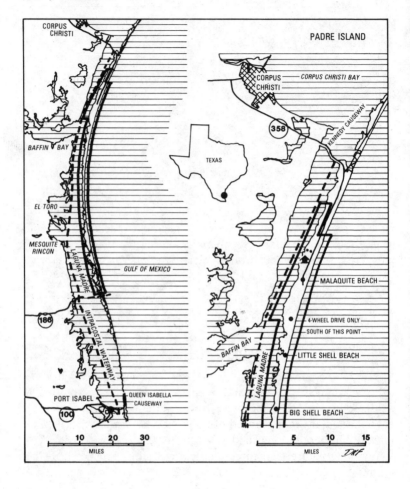

and other mollusks. Waterfowl winter here. Resident birds include white and brown pelicans, common and snowy egrets, great blue herons, gulls, at least four species of terns, and the magnificent frigate bird. From the mammal world are jackrabbits, coyotes, and spotted ground squirrels.

A few groves of scrub live oak adorn the island, but mostly it's occupied by sea oats, croton, beach evening-primrose, morning glory, and partridge pea. Surf fishing is excellent; so is beach-combing and treasure hunting.

To reach the Island: Take The John F. Kennedy Causeway out of Corpus Christi; from south end of island, take Queen Isabella Causeway from Port Isabel.

WHERE TO DRIVE

You can drive 14 miles southward from the northern boundary of the national seashore; you can drive on northward for approximately five miles from the southern end of the island, but you cannot reach the boundary of the national seashore. To do so, you must have a four-wheel-drive vehicle. Use caution not to molest wildlife while driving.

WHERE TO HIKE

The entire national seashore area is excellent for hiking, although in some places the sands are so soft as to make walking difficult. Along the tidewater areas, however, the sand is hard-packed. Do not enter any areas fenced off, however. No trails exist, but the terrain is generally open and you can make your own. A marked self-guiding nature trail three-quarters mile long is located in the seashore area.

BACKPACKING OPPORTUNITIES

Backpacking is permitted and during weekdays is excellent. This avoids heavier use on weekends and permits the backpacker to further his wilderness experience. No water is available, so you must carry your own. Also wear high-top shoes to keep sand out of your shoes.

WHERE TO CAMP

Primitive camping is permitted anyplace on the Gulf side of the national seashore area. Remember that in places there may be vehicle traffic along hard-packed beaches.

Where to Obtain Information

Superintendent
Padre Island Nat'l Seashore
Box 8560
Corpus Christi, TX 78412

OTHER AREAS TO CHECK

FOR ADDITIONAL—and in some cases limited—wilderness experiences not covered more extensively in this guidebook, consider the following:

APOSTLE ISLANDS, Lake Superior, Michigan: Contact Superintendent, 1972 Centennial Dr., Rural Route, Bayfield, WI 54814.

MCCORMICK TRACT, Michigan's Upper Peninsula: Contact Forest Supervisor, Ottawa National Forest, Ironwood, MI 49938.

PERE MARQUETTE RIVER, Michigan: Contact Dept. of Natural Resources, Steven T. Mason Bldg., Lansing, MI 48926.

PICTURED ROCKS NATIONAL LAKESHORE, Michigan: Contact P.O. Box 40, Munising, MI 49862.

WOLF RIVER, Wisconsin: Contact Dept. of Natural Resources, State Office Bldg., Madison, WI 53073.

BADLANDS NATIONAL MONUMENT, South Dakota: Contact Badlands National Monument, Wall, SD 57790.

BLACK HILLS, southwestern South Dakota: Contact Forest Supervisor, Black Hills National Forest, Custer, SD 57730.

LITTLE MIAMI RIVER, southwestern Ohio: Contact Dept. of Natural Resources, Fountain Square, Columbus, OH 43224.

LITTLE PINE CREEK, east central Ohio: Contact Bureau of Outdoor Recreation, 3853 Research Park Dr., Ann Arbor, MI 48104.

BEALL WOODS, southeastern Illinois along Wabash River: Contact Beall Woods State Park, Rochester, IL 62563.

BLACK RIVER, southeastern Missouri: Contact Missouri Conservation Comm., North Ten Mile Dr., Jefferson City, MO 65101.

FORT NIOBRARA, north central Nebraska: Contact Refuge Manager, Ft. Niobrara Wildlife Refuge, Valentine, NE 69201.

NIOBRARA RIVER from Pine Ridge to Fort Niobrara National Wildlife Refuge in north central Nebraska: Contact Nebraska Dept. of Economic Development, P.O. Box 94666, State Capitol, Lincoln, NE 68509.

KANZA PRAIRIE near Junction City, Kansas, 916 acres of unplowed bluestem prairie: Contact Kansas State University Endowment Assoc., Manhattan, KA 66506.

YELLOW CLIFF, Daniel Boone National Forest, Kentucky: Contact Forest Supervisor, Daniel Boone National Forest, Winchester, KY 40391.

OBED RIVER, Tennessee: Contact Bureau of Outdoor Recreation, 148 Cain St., Atlanta, GA 30303.

BUFFALO RIVER, Tennessee: Contact Bureau of Outdoor Recreation, 148 Cain St., Atlanta, GA 30303.

BUFFALO RIVER, Arkansas: Contact Buffalo National River, Box 1173, Harrison, AK 72601.

NOXUBEE WILDLIFE REFUGE, Brooksville, Mississippi: Contact Noxubee National Wildlife Refuge, Brooksville, MS 39739.